I0050919

Essentials of Cyber Security

PARADIGM BOOKS

Academic

Dhillon
Enterprise Cyber Security. Principles
and Practice

Hunter and Dhanda
Information Systems: The Challenges
of Theory and Practice

Hunter and Dhanda
Information Systems: Exploring
applications in business and
government

Wenn and Dhanda
Engaging Executive IS Practice

Hunter and Wenn
Information Systems in an E-World

Dhillon
Security Challenges in the New
Millennium

Wenn and Dhanda
Enabling Executive Information
Technology Competencies

Kamel and Irani
Information Technologies for
Organizational Enhancement

Irani and Kamel
Improving Business Performance
through Knowledge Management

Dhillon and Sa-Soares
Issues in protecting intangible
organizational assets

Dhillon and Sarin
Facing the Information Society

Hunter and Burgess
Grand Challenges in Business and
Information Management Processes

Dhanda and Hackney
Engaging Academia and Enterprise
Agendas

Sa-Soares
Social and Ethical Impact of
Technology

Dhanda and Hunter
Grand Challenges in Technology
Management

General Interest

Sharma
Maverick of success

Dhillon
The Inner Truth

Nand
Partition

Bhullar
The Enquiring Guru. Questions by the
Sikh Gurus and their answers

Essentials of Cyber Security

Gurpreet Dhillon, PhD

Virginia Commonwealth University, USA

Paradigm Books

Published by Paradigm Books and imprint of Aldwych Associates
2020 Pennsylvania Avenue NW, Ste 904
Washington DC 20006, USA
books@aldwychassociates.com

Copyright © 2014 by Gurpreet S. Dhillon. All right reserved.

All rights reserved. Under Title 17, U.S. Code, International and Pan-American Copyright Conventions. No part of this book may be reproduced by any means, electronic or mechanical, including photocopying, scanning, recording or duplication in whole or part by any information storage or retrieval systems without prior written permission from the author(s) and publisher(s), except for the inclusion of brief quotations with attribution in a review or report.

Paradigm Books does not exercise editorial control over books. Sole responsibility for the content of each work rests with the author(s) and/or contributing publisher(s) and not with Paradigm Books. Opinions expressed herein may not be interpreted in any way as representing those of Paradigm Books, nor of its affiliates.

Made and printed in USA
Typeset in Palatino
ISBN-13: 978-0692218006 (Paradigm Books)
ISBN-10: 0692218009

This book is dedicated to those who inspired me to read. Motivated me to write. Challenged me to think beyond the ordinary. And create a path where none existed. Mom, Dad – this is for you.

CONTENTS

Acknowledgements

Over the years, I have taught at several institutions around the world. I have held academic appointments in UK, Portugal, Hong Kong, Sweden and the USA. One aspect that I have enjoyed is interacting with my students. They have been refreshing, thought provoking and intellectually stimulating. My interactions with the students have often resulted in simplifying the concepts for easy consumption. Knowledge, after all, should be easy to gain and fun to digest. This book is one product of a series of such interactions. My sincere thanks to my students who allowed me to interact with them, pick their brains and often learn something new from the discourse.

Preface

Back in the day when I was a doctoral student, the only thing we knew of was "computer security". The use of terms such as "information security", "information systems security", were beginning to take hold. The use of the terms "cyber security" is more recent. One day I was asked to make a presentation to fellow doctoral students and faculty at the London School off Economics. A person, Perter Sommer, was in the audience. He was the famed author of the "Hacker's Handbook", which he had written under the pen name of Hugo Cornwall. As I was presenting my concepts and assertions, Peter raised and asked a very simple question. He said, "How do you define computer security?" A simple question it might have been. It, however, got me started on a journey. A journey spanning nearly two decades in the search to understand what we mean by "computer security".

The question I often ask myself is, "Do I have an answer to that fundamental question." Honestly speaking I probably have a partial answer. My exploration has led me to study Semiotics, the study of signs and sign processing. I ventured into reading "The Name of the Rose" by Umberto Eco and his more serious work, "The Theory of Semiotics". These works left a profound impact on me, my thinking and my conceptualizations. The journey offered an interesting insight: Can one understand what "computer" (or any of its variants) security is without appreciating it's ontological origins? And something must exist before other things can exist. Therefore, any understanding of security needs to be conceptualized in the context of what organizations are and how information systems get defined. In my 1997 book I note:

> Information system security concerns not just the security of the technical edifice but also that of the formal and informal systems within an organization. Hence the management of information system security goes beyond the relatively focused concerns for the

integrity of data held in a data management system (the technical system, i.e. computer based information system). Rather, it connotes the maintaining of a set of values. We speak of a person of integrity where that person is incorruptible, where they are able to retain the completeness of the system of values to which they aspire to embody. In this sense avoiding unauthorized modification of data in a computer based system is only part of the information system security concern. Equally important, if not more so, is the consistency with which decisions are taken, and the concordance between these decisions and the overall objectives of the organization. Here we take into account the consideration given by the members of the organization to the spirit behind the letter of regulations in the performance of routine tasks. In this sense information system security also relates to the consistency with which members interpret data and apply that interpretation to inform their decision making. Hence where there is a discordance between on the one hand the formally specified systems of authority, of information use, and on the other hand those that exist informally, in practice, then the integrity and security of the whole structure is threatened.

This book, hence, is an exploration. An exploration into the multiple facets of security. I have aptly titled it the "essentials of cyber security". It means many of the aspects covered in the book present the multiple facets of security. I hope you enjoy the text and welcome you to join me on my journey to explore what "computer" security is?

Gurpreet Dhillon, PhD
Richmond, Virginia, USA

One

1. Introduction to Cyber Security

The Basics

In recent years security of computer systems has become central to any business organization. The purpose of computer security is to ensure that the valuable resources of a firm remain protected. Such protection is instituted through appropriate safeguards. In most cases, safeguards are put in place to protect the financial information, reputation of the firm, personally identifiable information, legal position of the firm, trade secrets, among others.

Security of computer systems also ensures that the integrity of business processes is maintained. For instance, it is important to ensure that there is no disruption in the supply chain logistics. It is equally important that business processes are not broken. The overall security of operations is largely dependent on the integrity of data. This means that data residing in various computer systems and databases in an enterprise does not get changed, intentionally or unintentionally.

Computer security also ensures that the resources are made available to the right people at the right time. In case these are not, there can be disruptions in the operations of the firm. Inability to have the right access to data and information would result in inadequate or flawed decision-making. Non-availability of information typically is a consequence of both intentional as well as unintentional compromises. When data or information is unavailable because of intentional reasons, it is possibly because someone – a human or a machine – is a hurdle in the process. When data or information is unavailable because of intentional reasons, it is typically because of errors – human as well as logical.

Computer security therefore is really the protection of information resources of the firm. Protection is accomplished by ensuring confidentiality, integrity, and availability of data and information.

National Institute of Standards and Technology Perspective

The protection afforded to an automated information system in order to attain the applicable objectives of preserving the integrity, availability and confidentiality of information system resources (includes hardware, software, firmware, information/data, and telecommunications).

Source: NIST Special Publication 800-12, http://csrc.nist.gov/publications/nistpubs/800-12/

While ensuring **confidentiality**, **integrity**, and **availability** of data and information are indeed the core requirements of computer security, there are several other aspects that need careful consideration. The very function of maintaining confidentiality cannot be executed unless we are able to define what we mean by identity. In the realm of computer-based systems, there is no doubt that one needs to ensure the condition of being oneself or itself, and not another. Alongside, there is also a need to ensure that the person one claims to be, is indeed the one. This adds the requirement of **authenticity** to the protection of a firms' resource.

2

In the interconnected world that we live in, information resources of a firm are never located or stored in one place. This means that there is a constant movement of the information resources across various boundaries – firms, networks and countries. It is absolutely important, therefore, to ensure that the data and the information do not change as it moves from one location to the other. Hence it becomes important to ensure **non-repudiation**.

Core Concepts of Computer Security

Confidentiality: All data and information is kept private and is not disclosed to unauthorized individuals.

Integrity: All data and information is timely, accurate, complete and consistent.

Availability: Assurance that all data and information is available when required and that there is no denial of service.

Computer-based system vulnerabilities

Over the past few years there has been a consistent increase in the number and complexity of reported cyber threats. Symantec recently reported a nearly 81 percent increase in malicious attacks, with some 232 million identities stolen (Symantec, 2012). The report also notes a consistent increase in Advanced Persistent Threats (APTs). In 2011 alone, there were some 82 targeted attacks per day. The cyber threat landscape is clearly of significant concern. Internet based cyber threats, however, are not the only ones that are a cause of concern. Other kinds of threats are equally damaging. In general, threats fall into one the following six categories:

- Automated attacks (e.g. Botnets)
- Malicious intent cyber attacks (e.g. those on critical infrastructure)
- Internal employee cyber attacks
- Cyber attacks because of social engineering

- Loss of privacy and identity related attacks
- Cyber espionage related attacks

While all these types of attacks are inter-related, they all have a certain set of characteristics that distinguish them as categories in themselves. In paragraphs below we briefly discuss each category of cyber attacks.

For more Information, please explore the following resources:

http://goo.gl/kvQPm8

http://www.jissec.org

http://csis.org/category/topics/technology/cybersecurity

http://en.wikipedia.org/wiki/Computer_security

Automated attacks. Automated attacks can cause havoc since these can go unnoticed for long periods of time. There is no doubt that humans are at the origin of all automated attacks, but once propagated, human involvement is rather limited. Hackers are typically very fond of automated attacks, particularly SQL injection and Remote File Inclusion. This is because they are useful in exploiting website vulnerabilities. Over the years automated attacks have become rather sophisticated and there are several pieces of software available for exploitation – sqlmap, Havji, NetSparker, among others.

There are four main reasons why automated attacks are a vehicle of choice:

1. The tools require little technological prowess.

2. The tools are often freely available (from hacker sites or from legitimate penetration testing businesses).

3. The tools allow hackers to attack a vast number of sites rather quickly.

4. The tools make an efficient use of compromised and rented servers.

Automated attacks ⟶ **VULNERABILITY** ⟵ *Social Engineering*

Malicious intent ⟶ ⟵ *Privacy compromise*

Insider attack ⟶ ⟵ *Espionage*

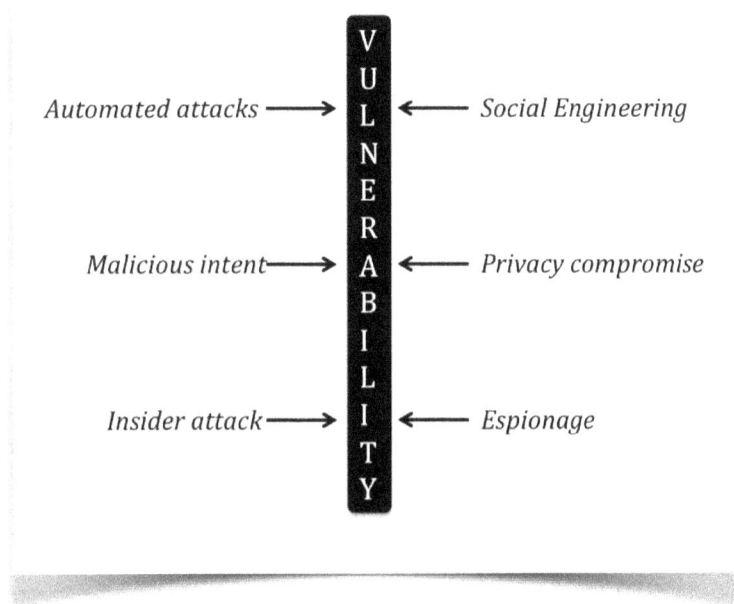

Figure 1.1, Computer system vulnerabilities

Malicious intent cyber attacks. Malicious intent cyber attacks are the most talked about threats today. On February 3, 2013 the 47th Super Bowl was halted for nearly 34 minutes because of a blackout. The immediate response from the media was that of a possible cyber attack. The Federal Bureau of Investigation later confirmed that there was no "intelligence to indicate" that the blackout was because of malicious intent. It was soon discovered that there was some abnormality in the equipment inside the stadium, which caused the electrical system to partially cut the power. However, proponents of critical infrastructure protection widely believe that the possibility of blackouts or attacks on utilities are indeed real. There needs to be some level of individual responsibility to ensure protection.

SQL Injection

In rather simple terms a Standard Query Language Injection arises because the fields available for users to input their data also allow SQL statements to pass through. This typically allows querying the database directly. Since the websites by nature are open to the public, security mechanisms allow all web traffic to communicate with web application. This is generally over port 80/443). The web application will usually have open access to the database so that it is able to return requested information. SQL Injection attacks occur because of inadequate system designs.

Remote File Inclusion

A Remote File Inclusion (RFI) attack is one where an attacker is able to upload a malicious file on a service. This is usually accomplished through a script. Vulnerability is exploited because there is possibly a poor validation check. Improper checks allow for a code to be executed either on the website or on the server (e.g. cross site scripting (XSS) attack using JavaScript).

The US Department of Homeland Security has reported that in 2012 there were at least 82 attacks on the energy sector, 29 on the water industry, 7 on chemical plants and 6 on nuclear companies. The magnitude and the targeted sites make such kinds of cyber attacks a serious cause of concern (DHS, 2012).

Threats to national infrastructure are global in nature. In March 2013, several South Korean banks and television broadcasters went offline because of a series of cyber attacks by North Korea (CBS News, 2013). Similar occurrences have been reported in Saudi Arabia, Israel, India, with blame being attributed on several rogue nations. Whosoever may be really behind the attacks on critical infrastructures, the problem exists and needs to be dealt with.

In the Middle East, Cyber attacks are Flavored with Political Rhetoric

In the beginning of January, a self-described Saudi Arabian hacker known only by the handle 0xOmar claimed he had posted details of 400,000 Israeli credit cards online. The target was commercial assets, but the message of the attack was political: In online statements he said that he belonged to "the largest Wahhabi hacker group of Saudi Arabia," that counted among its targets credit card accounts used to donate to "Israeli Zionist Rabbis." It was the first salvo in a series of attacks the regional press has come to describe as "cyber warfare" between Arab and Israeli hackers this month.

Days after his first leak, 0xOmar posted online another information batch of 11,000 Israeli credit cardholders, though Israeli banks said altogether only 20,000 credit card accounts had been compromised. Soon after, an Israeli hacker calling himself '0xOmer' went online to announce he had posted names, email addresses, phone numbers and credit information of 217 Saudi Arabian credit cardholders. 0xOmar promptly released online the information of another 200 Israeli cardholders, and upped his rhetoric.

More Arab credit card accounts were posted online in response, and the hacking then moved on to larger commercial targets, as the websites of the Tel Aviv Stock Exchange, El Al Airlines and several Israeli banks were disrupted. Israeli hackers responded, attacking the Abu Dhabi Securities Exchange and Tadawul, Saudi Arabia's exchange, then the United Arab Emirates' Central Bank website and that of the Arab Bank Palestine. The Israeli hackers said their actions were also politically motivated. "You can call this a Zionist revenge," the hackers told Israeli newspaper Yedioth Ahronoth.

The incidents highlight the ability of cyber criminals to carry out attacks across borders, even when corporations are aware of their threats. They also demonstrate how digital disruptions could become a tool in state conflict. The Middle East is considered a boom market for cyber security; according to RNCOS research, the regional market for IT security software is expected to grow at a CAGR of over 34% from 2010 to 2013. But the mixing of historical political disputes with cybercrime and cyber vandalism gives online threats in the region a distinct tinge.

"The question that then arises is how can organizations and individuals protect themselves," says Gurpreet Dhillon, professor of information security at Virginia Commonwealth University. "It is no longer the question of buying an ever so complex lock. It is more about ensuring that the key to the lock is not compromised. Part of the exercise is about awareness. Many of the social engineering attacks go unnoticed because individuals do not know about the nature and scope of the attack. Many organizations are also ill-prepared to deal with cyber threats."

Source: Knowledge@Wharton. (2012). In the Middle East, cyberattacks are flavored with political rhetoric.

Retrieved from http://knowledge.wharton.upenn.edu/arabic/article.cfm?articleid=2774. Excerpt reproduced with permission.

Internal employee cyber attacks. Ever since the dependence of businesses on information and communication technologies, threats posed by internal employees have been of great significance. There are several reasons why internal employees subvert controls. Based on extensive research, Dhillon (2001) identifies three reasons why employees engage in such acts:

- Personal circumstances
- Work situations
- Opportunities

Typically, companies tend to ignore the personal factors of employees. In fact, these are one of the main reasons why employees may engage in illicit activities. Personal factors may range from financial hardships to sour relationships. The psychological pressure caused by personal factors can have a significant impact on deviant behavior.

Work situations are also a major factor for people to engage in behaviors that cause damage to the information assets of a firm. Hostile relationships with a boss or being denied a promotion can result in an employee being disgruntled. Such employees do nothing but cause havoc. There are several known cases where internal employees have planted viruses or other logical bombs just because they were disgruntled and unhappy with the way they had been treated.

Finally, opportunities that any workplace may offer can be a source of a threat. Such opportunities largely arise because of broken processes or other flaws in software development. It is usually the internal employees who know where the vulnerabilities are and how these could be subverted.

This was succinctly illustrated through the WikiLeaks saga, which resulted in Jacob Lew, Director of the Office of Management and Budget of the United States, to issue a memorandum on safeguarding information and counterintelligence postures (Lew, 2010).

Cyber attacks because of social engineering. A social engineering attack in its simplest form is a way in which a victim is tricked to respond to a series of questions. Such questions may be sought over a phone or the victim may be directed to a certain website. The intent is to gain as much information about the victim or the victim's organization such that there is a higher chance of breaking into computer systems with the acquired information. Typically users are tricked so that they self-infect their computers with some malware. Social engineering attacks come in different guises. The most common forms include breaking news alerts, greeting cards, bogus lottery winnings. The majority of social engineering attacks play on the natural desire of individuals to take advantage of a good deal. As the old adage goes, "if something is too good to be true, it probably is a scam".

Loss of privacy and identity related attacks

Identity theft occurs when someone steals credentials of a person and uses them without permissions. Such credentials could include Social Security Numbers, credit card details, among others. When an individual assumes identity of another person, an impersonation fraud occurs. The theft of individual identification and use of the credentials is in most cases used to rent apartments, apply for credit cards. Such frauds are commonly reported in the media. In recent years, however, there has been a growing trend to use individually identifying information to seek medical treatment and bilk insurers through fake claims. In years to come, medical frauds of this kind are expected to grow exponentially.

Cyber espionage related attacks. In March 2012, the Economist published a survey on attitudes towards cyber theft. In the survey 82% of the respondents felt that cyber espionage is clearly illegal and that national and international authorities should be involved in combating with the problem. At the same time nearly 78% felt that stopping cyber espionage was a shared responsibility. And 61% felt that cyber espionage cases were underreported (Economics, 2012).

For more Information, please explore the following resources:

CNBC. (2008). Dhillon on security and privacy: Breaking the system. Retrieved from http://www.youtube.com/watch?v=Ji5DDbLpTUg

The video by Gurpreet Dhillon (see picture) discusses how easy it is to compromise privacy and personally identifiable information. The video brings home the point that identity is tangible and that it's loss can be devastating.

https://www.youtube.com/watch?v=3WUo9h7QF_M

This video is by IBM and explores and presents the top trends in identity and access management

https://www.youtube.com/watch?v=0NFanER0g8w

This is a video by Ian Glazer (see picture, who has done some amazing work in the area while at Gartner)

Federal Trade Commission. (2007). Deter, Detect, Defend against identity theft. Retrieved from http://www.youtube.com/watch?v=7AHORRN5wC0

This video discusses issues related to identity compromises. Identity compromises are certainly on an increase and are a topic of concern and are increasingly a topic of discussion.

In recent months, there have been a barrage of accusations between US and China about the role played by certain technology firms in industrial and national cyber espionage. In particular, Huawei Technologies Company was singled out by the US. On March 28, 2013, the US government demanded oversight of network-equipment purchases, if it were to approve the acquisition of US phone carrier Sprint Nextel by SoftBank. Suspicions abound that Huawei Technologies works with the Chinese government and is involved in cyber espionage.

Whatever the reality of exchanges between nation states and companies, the problem of cyber espionage is real and theft of intellectual property, including national secrets, is of a significant concern

Safety of systems and data

Going forward any cyber security strategy requires a blueprint focusing on innovation and prosperity, balancing economic and national security interests and integrating privacy and civil liberty interests.

Innovation and prosperity through cyber security. There is a fine balance between usability of systems and security. Companies cannot afford to institute such a high level of security so that the systems are difficult to use. At the heart of the problem is a rather simple issue – appropriate use of technology. The question usually does not just relate to what is the best available technology to solve a given problem. The question is, what is the most appropriate technology for the solution. The use of "best" technology may result in affecting a plethora or other structural and procedural issues – perhaps at times over-engineering the solutions. There is no doubt then that there is constant conflict between innovation and prosperity. As a business, there is a need to innovate such that new products and services can be brought to the market. Businesses also need to innovate and contain costs. Yet the technological solutions may curtail prosperity. Technological advances of sorts may also challenge the usability principles. This is because several layers of controls may have to be put in place.

On March 28, 2013 the Wall Street Journal ran a story of a small business in Virginia Beach attempting to use technology for ordering cupcakes at a bakery. The motivation was largely because of high labor costs. However, the nature of software development and the related controls that will have to be instituted would over complicate the solution and may perhaps make the system too difficult to use.

So, some careful consideration is required to balance innovation and prosperity, security and usability, over-engineering and appropriateness of use of technology.

Balancing economic and national security interests. With respect to balancing economic and national interests in the context of cyber security, Huawei Technologies of China is a perfect case in point. The US has repeatedly claimed that Huawei-made telecommunication equipment is designed to allow unauthorized access by China.

US Secretary of Defense Leon Panetta speaking ion the issue in 2012

"These attacks mark a significant escalation of the cyber threat and they have renewed concerns about still more destructive scenarios that could unfold. For example, we know that foreign cyber actors are probing America's critical infrastructure networks. They are targeting the computer control systems that operate chemical, electricity and water plants and those that guide transportation throughout this country. We know of specific instances where intruders have successfully gained access to these control systems. We also know that they are seeking to create advanced tools to attack these systems and cause panic and destruction and even the loss of life.

Let me explain how this could unfold. An aggressor nation or extremist group could use these kinds of cyber tools to gain control of critical switches. They could, for example, derail passenger trains or even more dangerous, derail trains loaded with lethal chemicals. They could contaminate the water supply in major cities or shutdown the power grid across large parts of the country. The most destructive scenarios involve cyber actors launching several attacks on our critical infrastructure at one time, in combination with a physical attack on our country. Attackers could also seek to disable or degrade critical military systems and communication networks.

The collective result of these kinds of attacks could be a cyber Pearl Harbor; an attack that would cause physical destruction and the loss of life. In fact, it would paralyze and shock the nation and create a new, profound sense of vulnerability. As director of the CIA and now Secretary of Defense, I have understood that cyber attacks are every bit as real as the more well-known threats like terrorism, nuclear weapons proliferation and the turmoil that we see in the Middle East." See: http://www.defense.gov/

In spite of Huawei moving its headquarters to the UK, the British government raised doubts about the company and the equipment. The Indian Department of Telecommunications blocked the company from supplying equipment to India's Bharat Sanchar Nigam Limited (BSNL). The Australian government excluded Huawei from tendering to bid for the National Broadband Network. While Huawei has consistently denied its linkages to the Chinese government and it denied any involvement in national espionage efforts, other nation states have taken a stance of sacrificing short term economic benefits in light of national security interests. Balancing such interests is going to gain significant importance in years to come (see Cusick. (2012).

Integrating privacy and civil liberties. There is no doubt that strengthening privacy and civil liberties is of utmost importance. The issue is of concern usually is the fear that the government may collect information and use it for potentially inappropriate purposes – political, law enforcement, administrative actions etc. Opinions are divided if, post 9/11, the collection of massive amounts of information without judicial or congressional oversight was justified. However, because of weak consumer privacy protection in the US and governments' surveillance activities, there seems to be little confidence in state-sponsored cyber security initiatives. Clearly significant confidence building is necessary if privacy and civil liberties are to be adequately integrated.

PRIVACY AND CIVIL LIBERTIES OVERSIGHT BOARD

The Privacy and Civil Liberties Oversight Board is specifically tasked with providing oversight of such issues. For instance see their report: http://www.pclob.gov/SiteAssets/Pages/default/PCLOB-Report-on-the-Telephone-Records-Program.pdf

Summary

In this chapter we have examined the top threats to a network. We have also evaluated the nature and scope of attacks on a network. The application of key cyber security techniques to problematic areas is also considered. The chapter identifies and suggests online cyber security protection resources.

Two

2. Cyber Stalking, Fraud and Abuse

The Basics

Stalking refers to the unwanted attention by an individual or a group and typically results in harassment and intimidation. Unlike traditional stalking where people are harassed by physical actions, **cyberstalking** makes use of internet and other electronic devices for harassment. In September 2012, the Bureau of Justice Statistics (BJS) released a report on stalking cases in the United States. According to the report, the most vulnerable people are young adults and women and the damage could range from physical abuse, to loss of jobs, vandalism, financial loss, identity theft and even assault and murder (Catalano, 2012).

Stalking has several implications and could also lead to psychological trauma and personal loss. Cyberstalking, however, has added a new dimension to persecution and make victims feel a palpable sense of fear. Prosecution of criminals is challenging as stalkers can fake their identities or can choose to be anonymous. This makes it difficult for the victim and cyber police to track them down. Lack of internet regulations, and the nascence of computer forensics has given stalkers a kind of free hand. Moreover, the rapid evolution of technology leads to the advent of new cyberstalking practices, making it more difficult for victims and cyber police to identify and punish a perpetrator

While cyberstalking can come in many forms, the most common tactics of a cyber-stalker include:

- Threatening, harassing or manipulative emails sent out from various accounts
- Hacking on personal information and gaining access to victims personal records or accounts
- Creating fake accounts on social networking sites to gain information about victim or connect or lure victims
- Posting information about victim on different forums that cause victim embarrassment, loss of reputation or financial loss
- Signing up different forums using victims credentials
- Seeking privileges such as loan approvals using victim information

In the US several states have enacted Cyberstalking and Cyber harassment laws. One of the more recent perils of the Cyber Stalking laws was the *Petraeus Affair*. FBI began investigating Paula Broadwell for sending allegedly harassing emails to Jill Kelley. One of the apparent problems emerging from the Petraeus affair case was the fact that majority of the laws are written for speech rather than intimidation or harassment. The Petraeus affair details can be found at: http://goo.gl/DwVBy

For more Information, please explore the following resources:

For a complete listing of the laws visit:

http://goo.gl/KVhjR4

Privacy Rights Clearinghouse. (2013). Fact sheet 14: Are you being stalked? Retrieved from https://www.privacyrights.org/fs/fs14-stk.htm

Catalano, S. (2012, September). Stalking victims in the United States – revised. U.S. Department of Justice, Bureau of Justice Statistics. Retrieved from http://bjs.gov/content/pub/pdf/svus_rev.pdf

---

The nature and scope of Cyberstalking

According to Merritt (2013) cyberstalking covers a range of crimes that involve the use of internet as one of the primary facets mediums to engage in a range of criminal activities - false accusations, monitoring, threats, identity theft, data destruction or manipulation and exploitation of minor).

Recently a case from Hyattsville, Maryland came to light where a man was found guilty of 73 counts of stalking. It included reckless endangerment, harassment and violation of a protective order. In this case the victim of an individual's ex-wife who reportedly endured almost 45 days of online harassment. The accused kept sending threatening emails, created false profiles of the victim using her real name, and invited men to come visit her at home. Oddly the accused denied having committed a crime, but the harassing behavior stopped upon his arrest. It is a known fact that angry spouses or lovers perpetrate most of the crimes. Various surveys also show that in 60% of the cases victims are females (see Ginty, 2011).

Figure 2.1, "Revenge Porn" is emerging to be a new menace

In recent years "revenge porn" has also emerged as a new menace (Figure 2.1). This is when ex partners post sexually explicit photos on websites. Various calls are currently being made for stricter laws that are specifically aimed at stopping revenge porn.

Another recent example highlights the effect of cyberstalking on the victim. In 2012, Patrick Macchione was sentenced to four years in prison and 15 years of probation for cyberstalking a college classmate. One thing in particular to note from this case is that the perpetrator started the online relationship in a seemingly normal manner. After gathering enough information for the stalking such as the victim's cell phone number and place of employment, his interactions with her became increasingly harassing. At one point the victim was receiving 30 to 40 calls in a five-hour work shift and the perpetrator would appear at her place of employment and in one instance even chased her vehicle. His interactions included text messages, Facebook and twitter harassment as well as in person contact, demanding affection from the victim and threatening violence if his demands weren't met. In this case the victim continues to fear that her perpetrator will find a way to come after her and becomes anxious if she receives too many messages or text messages in a short period of time.

Even those in the military can become infatuated enough with an individual to stalk them. A member of the United States Navy was convicted of cyberstalking a former girlfriend. Notable in his case was use of GPS technologies to track her location using her cell phone signal as well as somehow managing to get monitoring software on her computer to view her online activities. At one point he went as far as to create a fake Facebook profile under another name so that he could continue to observe her Facebook related activity after she successfully got a retraining order against him. Prior to sentencing, the perpetrator underwent psychiatric evaluation to ensure that he could be held accountable for the crimes (CBS8, 2011).

Sometimes, the aftermath of a cyberstalking incident goes beyond just mental and emotional harm and includes violence against the victim. Last summer, an entire family was indicted on cyberstalking and murder charges when they conspired to harm and eventually murdered a woman that was divorcing a family member and pushing for custody of the children involved in the relationship. The family utilized social media websites as well as YouTube in a "campaign to ruin [the victim's] reputation" (Garcia, 2013). A false website was also created to attempt to sway public opinion regarding the victim in hopes of currying favor after their planned murder of her. At one point, there were additional friends who were providing information back to the family such as license plate numbers and photos of the victim's home.

Status Report – Cyberbullying

In recent years, cyberbullying has become a serious issue around the world as a result of social media. This type of bullying occurs by the use of any type of electronic technology, and is extremely difficult to overcome. According to stopbullying.gov, the 2008-2009 School Crime Supplement from the National Center for Education Statistics and Bureau of Justice Statistics indicated that six percent of students in middle and high school had experienced cyberbullying. Furthermore, a 2011 risk behavior survey conducted on students in grades 9-12 found that 16% had been electronically bullied within the previous year.

Cyberbullying is a problem that does not have a shelf life. It can occur daily for weeks, months, and years. More troubling is the ease by which children and even adults employ technology for the purpose of bullying. With the click of a button, individuals can post threatening, embarrassing or mean photos and statements about others through social media, text messages, or other means of technology.

Fortunately, there are ways to curb cyberbullying. First, the person must recognize that he or she is being cyberbullied, and should refuse to respond to the threat. Next, he or she should make a copy or take a screen shot of the threat. This will help to back up the claim when sent in to the website for a complaint, or when taking the threat to the local police department, if it is serious enough. If the local police department does not have a cyber crimes department, or it is so serious a threat that it warrants federal notification, one should take the threat forward to the Internet Crime Complaint Center (IC3), a division run by the Federal Bureau of Investigation (FBI), the National White Collar Crime Center, and the Bureau of Justice Assistance . To further ensure security, people need to set their social network information to the highest security level possible, and consider changing passwords on these sites as well as email programs.

Contributed by Jenna Hartzell. Source: http://www.facebook.com/securereview

Contact over the internet is an additional level removed from in-person contact and is often less inhibitive in nature. Unfortunately, this means that people who may have negative feelings are more likely to cyberstalk than physically stalk an individual. Coupled with the fact that cyberstalking cases often cost victims more than double when compared to standard stalking cases (Kuhles, 2013), the cost of cyberstalking to society will be much greater than traditional stalking economically, socially and emotionally.[1]

Social Networking Sites and Cyberstalking

A **social networking site** is a web-based service that allows people to connect and share resources. Popular social networking sites include but not limited to Facebook, Twitter, and LinkedIn. Social networking sites have emerged as a new communication phenomenon. However, given the wide accessibility, social networking sites contribute to novel or previously unknown risks. According to National Center for Victims of Crime website, most of social networking sites don't validate authenticity of user profiles and once a member, a person can post and access any kind of information (Stalking Resource Center). While some controls are provided, the user safety depends on how much a user knows about those controls and who all has access to the information.

Although use of social networking sites requires a member to agree to moral conduct; the enforcement of terms is sporadic at best. The fatal attraction of ever expanding connections and profile pages which display autobiographies, and opportunities for self-advertisement to an unhealthy degree can lead members to ignore the pitfalls of these websites. The Pew Research Center reports that 55% of online teens have a profile on social networking sites and 77% of these are shared profiles. Of those users who have shared online profiles, 59% say that their profile is visible only to their friends whereas 40% say that their profile is publicly available and just 1% of social network users are unsure about their profile visibility (Lenhart &

---

[1] Many thanks to our student Brian Rhodes for his contributions to this section.

Madden, 2007).

Stalkers take advantage of information available openly. Information such as person's birth date, location, likes, favorite bands, connections, work details, educational institutes can be used in various ways to exploit a victim. The information may be used to guess passwords, seek acquaintances, or even cause personal harm. In case the information is not accessible directly, stalkers fake their identity and pose as someone who they are not. As posted on the website of Federal Bureau of Investigation, fake profiles come in all forms for example, "Adults posing as children who are about the same age as the victim who later travel to abuse the child" (FBI, Social Networking, n.d.)

Some most recent and dreadful cases of cyberstalking:

Michigan man charged with cyberstalking and attempted sexual exploitation of minor victims. Retrieved from

http://www.fbi.gov/buffalo/press-releases/2012/michigan-man-charged-with-cyberstalking-and-attempted-sexual-exploitation-of-minor-victims

---

Over the last few years, several cases of stalking via social networking sites have gained public attention. It is not only the teenagers who can fall victim, people of all ages and groups are vulnerable. As reported by Science Daily, the research based on the 2006 Supplemental Victimization Survey from the National Criminal Crime Victimization Survey shows that approximately 70 percent of the victims of cyberstalking are women, while female victims only represented 58 percent in cyberstalking cases. In addition, average age for stalking victims is 40.8 years old, while cyberstalking victims averaged 38.4 years old (Science Daily, 2013).

The best defense against cyberstalking is to use Internet and social networking with responsibility. Making sensitive information available for public views can increase the vulnerability. Before posting or exchanging any information, one needs to think who really can have access to information and how the information can be exploited. Some simple measures include:

1. Limit online exchange of sensitive information such as financial details; instead call the person and provide the details

2. Never friend a 10 minute acquaintance; limit your online "friends" to people you actually know in person

3. Set your privacy settings to highest

4. Never post the pictures or images with identifiers such as school names etc.

5. And lastly, use caution and seek help if required

For more Information, please explore the following resources:

Stalking resource center. 2012. The National Center for Victims of Crime. Retrieved from http://goo.gl/WUojWm

FBI. Social Networking sites: Online friendships can mean offline peril. The Federal Bureau of Investigation. Retrieved from http://goo.gl/Wz5Z8M

Privacy right clearinghouse. https://www.privacyrights.org/are-you-being-stalked

Cyberbullying/Stalking & Harassment https://www.wiredsafety.org/subjects/cyberbullying.php

---

Fraud and Identity Theft

An unauthorized access to personal information without explicit consent of the person to whom it pertains is known as **identity theft**. Seeking and using someone's personal information for illicit financial gain is known as **identity fraud**. The personal information includes person first name, last name, social security number (SSN), address, banking details etc. The fraudster can use one or more of these personal identifiers to create a fake identity and seek privileges. As the Federal Bureau of Investigation puts it, identity theft is always committed to facilitate other crimes such credit card fraud, loan fraud, check fraud, and more (FBI, Identity theft, n.d.). Criminals either make use of the personal information by themselves or sell it online to highest bidder, which makes it harder for law enforcement to find the perpetrator. In a survey conducted by Federal Trade Commission (FTC) in 2006, 8.3 million Americans were reported to be the victims of identity theft and fraud and victims spent around 200 million hours in attempting to overcome identity fraud (FTC, 2007).

Computer intrusion significantly increases the impact and scope of identity theft. In one of the investigations in 1999, the FBI found that the computer network of an e-commerce company was compromised. The hacker demanded money from the company to stop him from posting the information publicly on the Internet. The fraud came to be known when several people complained of being charged an unauthorized amount on their accounts. According to a FBI report, 30 million credit card accounts and customer information was stolen. The customer information acquired through computer compromise was enough to create fake identities and further reuse those identities to secure loans and other privileges.

Some of the possible indications of identity fraud are

- Unauthorized charges appearing on account statement
- Denial of credit for poor credit score despite maintain a good credit history
- Contacted by creditors for payment of dues that you never acquired
- Not receiving regular bank statement
- Not receiving a renewed or replacement card

Identity theft is growing problem and is manifested in various ways. Some of the common forms of identity theft and related cybercrime include intrusion of third-party server to get credit card information, financial document, spams (mass emails) and phishing schemes. **Spam** is any kind of online communication initiated to engage in identity theft. Most of the spams appear to be an advertiser selling some kind of product or service, but some spams could be severely malicious. The intent is to attract victims to provide their personal information or to redirect to another website hosting malicious code or viruses to be installed on victims' computer for later use.

Phishing is another scheme to execute identity theft. It is an email message that appears to be sent by a legitimate source and asks for personal identifiable information. Basically, the criminals exploit the trust relationship that a victim has developed with an entity over the years. Typically, criminals spoof the email addresses and websites of trusted companies or government organizations and then ask the victims who interact with these organizations for personal information. Usually, the phishing criminals send out spam to millions of people and hence it could be a lucrative enterprise even if a very small percentage of victims respond by disclosing their personal financial information. In a growing number of cases, the crime involves international aspects as well. As stated by the FBI, international subjects solicit victims through social networking sites, job postings and chat rooms. Once the information is procured, criminals use it to post auctions on well-known auction websites. Funds are transferred through several accounts and the items sold are never delivered (Martinez, 2004).

One can take simple measures to prevent from being victimized by fraudsters in e-transactions:

- Use spam blocks and filter option
- Set the privacy setting to highest
- Do not reply to or click on suspiciously spam messages
- Don't download content attached with email; read the text first
- Read message subjects carefully
- Don't further forward spams to your friends
- Avoid simple email addresses
- Keep your personal information confidential
- Never post your personal information online

Scam watch resources

Federal Trade Commission maintains a "Scam Watch" page at:

http://goo.gl/AKJ7Yc

Watch "Protect yourself from Investment Scams"

http://youtu.be/TzwQ3dqv4mg

Investment Scams. With the advances in information and communication technologies, an interesting breed of scams has emerged. While the application domains can range from financial services, real estate to recruitment, the most interesting of these are in the area of sports. Typically sales people would try and sell some kind of prediction software. The sales pitch is that the system is foolproof and that there is guaranteed profit in <fill in the blank> - it could be horseracing, soccer, football or a multitude of other domains. The schemes can cost several thousand dollars and at times with an ongoing monthly payment.

Some of the interesting identity fraud cases:

FBI. (2005). Shampoo, Cut, Blow Dry . . . And a Fake ID: Salon owner and five others plead guilty in fraudulent ID racket. Federal Bureau of Investigation. Retrieved from http://www.fbi.gov/news/stories/2005/march/salon_032305

Hyde, J. (2013). Alleged Identity Theft and Credit Card Fraud Schemes Result in Charges Against 15 Individuals. Federal Bureau of Investigation. Retrieved from http://goo.gl/QdB9LE

Scammers make money because 1) the software was poorly designed and does not function as promised 2) the level of promised returns does not match expectations 3) the company does not exist and cannot be contacted after a certain period of time. Some common explanations offered in the sales pitch include:

Horseracing: There software purportedly predicts weather conditions, preparedness of the horse and the jockey. The software may also offer a money-tracking tool particularly how other professional betters may have invested.

Team Sport betting: The software offered proposes to help identify opportunities and trends. Various odds offered by bookmakers are considered. While the software as such may help accomplish some of the tasks, the quality of the logic may be questionable.

Share price prediction: Software that helps prediction of share prices and their movement may be offered. The quality and ability of the programmers to simulate real conditions is however questionable.

Summary

In this chapter we have evaluated various types of Internet scams and frauds. Specific steps required to avoid cyber fraud were also evaluated. Issues related with identity management and the related laws were discussed.

3. Denial of Service

The Basics

In the early 1960s, most computers within an organization existed in the form of giant Mainframe systems. These systems were centrally located within an organization and held all of the company's business data, performing all of the necessary calculations on this data. While mainframe systems are capable of handling very large quantities of data, they are also very expensive to build and manage. As the need for information to be processed faster and faster grew, companies had a difficult time aligning their IT budgets to meet these ambitious performance goals. Due to this, cheaper solutions were realized by replacing these costly systems with multiple, inexpensive computers that could be connected together. Over time, many mainframe systems began dissolving within organizations and were replaced with distributed environments.

The term distributed refers to multiple autonomous systems that communicate across a network with each other and work together to form a common goal. In its simplest form, distributed computing can be described as computing that is orchestrated between two or more computers. Each computer has its own local memory and information is exchanged between the systems by passing messages using the available communication link. Calculating extremely large numbers and complex algorithms can sometimes take minutes if not hours to complete on a single machine. Distributed computing can speed this process up by breaking large, complex equations into smaller subsets of calculations. These individual calculations are then sent off to each computer which in turn performs its necessary work. When all computers have finished, the individual solutions are then aggregated back together and a final answer is formed. To demonstrate, instead of one computer counting from 1-100, we could have ten computers counting ranges of ten (1-10, 11-20, etc). This is where distributed environments become extremely powerful and useful.

There are many different architectural approaches to the concept of distributed computing. One such model is the client-server approach in which a client receives data from the server, a user on the client-side views/ modifies this data, and (if a change occurred) the data is sent back to the server. Another form of the client-server model is almost the inverse of the previously described approach whereby a client sends data to the server. The server then performs the necessary calculations and, when the computations are finalized and the data is ready, it is sent back to the client. Distributed computing also exists as cloud computing, which has just recently started receiving attention by organizations and the media. It's important to note that with the first two models, the servers are usually owned by the organization. Yet in regards to the cloud concept, a third-party organization hosts the server and leases its computers out to organizations, performing calculations and storing data for them. The push for clouds is that the maintenance and control of these servers are abstracted away from the organization, which can instead focus on its business objectives instead of worrying about the technology that they use.

Knowledge Security

As we talk about knowledge, we need to determine its purpose and importance with an organization. To better understand its purpose, knowledge first needs to be formally defined. Merriam-Webster explains knowledge as the fact or condition of knowing something with familiarity gained through experience or association. Gaining knowledge is vital to an organization as a whole. This criticality comes from the fact that knowledge and knowing certain things are what sets an organization apart from others. Success often comes to the companies that have the best information and wield it in the most effective manner. The old adage holds that knowledge is power and, through this, knowledge breeds competition. As companies attempt to understand what their competitors know, they similarly want to defend and keep their knowledge secretive. The goal of an organization therefore is to maximize the amount of exclusive knowledge that they possess.

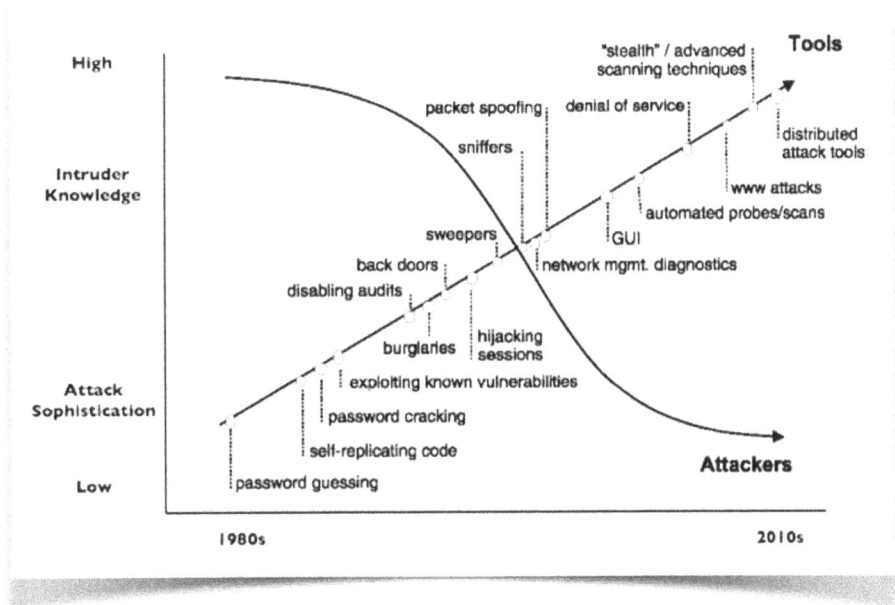

Figure 3.1, Attack sophistication over the years

A company must find effective ways of allowing their employees to share their knowledge and create a comprehensive body of knowledge that can be used throughout the company. However, this must also be done in a secure way. After all, once an organization's exclusive knowledge becomes available to their competitors, the advantage of being the sole owner of that information is lost. The sharing and protection of knowledge exists through the areas of knowledge management and knowledge security. As knowledge expansion occurs in an organization, we refer to the area of knowledge management - in which its purpose is to develop information internally to increase profit, instead of only having a few individuals with competitive knowledge. Upon the successful expansion of knowledge, information security is applied to again keep the information private.

Denial of Service attacks

A **denial of service** attack (DoS) is defined as an act to make one or more computer systems unavailable. By being unavailable the system cannot perform its normal function, whether that function is taking orders for products by an online vendor, taking donations at a charity, or simply displaying information. DoS attack consumes the resources of a network or a website and prevents the legitimate users from accessing those resources. As noted by the United States Computer Emergency Readiness Team, the most common form of DoS attack occurs when an attacker sends large number of spurious requests to a website (US-CERT, n.d.). Since the website servers can handle limited number of requests at a point of time, the attacker overwhelms the servers with multiple requests. This causes the network to overload or crash and thus the legitimate users can't access the website.

Watch the following video for a summary of denial of service attacks:

CBT Nuggets. (2013, February 18). MicroNugget: What is a Distributed Denial of Service Attack? [video]. Retrieved from http://youtu.be/ B_28P85s-2s

---

There are two categories of denial of service attacks: **logic attack** and **flooding attack**. In the first class, logic attacks exploit the vulnerabilities of the software to cause the remote servers to crash. An example of this is the "ping of death," where the attacker sends an IP packet so large that the operating system crashes. In the second class, the attacker generates a large number of requests to flood the victim's resources, causing the servers to slow down and eventually crash. The most popular attacks include the **buffer overflow attacks**, **ICMP flood** and **SYN flood**.

Denial of service attacks can originate either from one machine, or, more commonly and effectively, from multiple machines. A multiple-machine denial of service is defined as a **distributed denial of service attack (DDoS)**. While DoS can cause significant damage by using a single machine, DDoS is capable of launching catastrophic attacks by using multiple machines. The ability to utilize the machines distributed across the world makes it difficult to trace the origin of the attack.

Usually the websites of high profile organizations are susceptible to DoS attacks. Various companies in the United States have experienced such attacks, including Bank of America, Wells Fargo, Amazon, Visa, MasterCard, and Yahoo. While attackers may succeed in compromising the sensitive information residing on company servers, the main intention of the attack is to make the organization's website inaccessible to its customers. It costs a victim a great deal of resources in terms of time and capital to overcome the attack. Moreover, the attack can lead to loss of reputation, trust and customers.

While there are various methods to execute DoS attacks, there are also many tools available to prevent or defend these attacks. Installing antivirus software, configuring firewalls and following security practices can reduce the likelihood a machine can be used to launch such attacks.

Denial of Service Attack Methods

There are various methods of executing denial of service attack. Some of the commonly known attacks include:

1.   **Bandwidth reap**:   In a typical bandwidth attack, the attacker floods the network beyond its bandwidth. By

exhausting the network bandwidth, the legitimate users may not get access to the resources. Usually, attackers use a large number of machines to generate bogus requests to overwhelm the network.

2.	**SYN attack**: SYN attack makes use of the TCP handshake process. The attacker sends the connection request (SYN). The victim responds back (SYN/ACK) and waits for the acknowledgement from sender (ACK). Since the attacker never sends the final acknowledgment, the victim's connection table fills up and consequently the legitimate users cannot gain access.

3.	**SMURF attack**: In Smurf attacks, the third party server attacks the victim server by acting as an unwitting proxy on behalf of attacker. This attack requires 3 machines; the attacker, the proxy and the victim. The attacker uses ICMP packets (level 3 ping) to proxy or intermediary machines with source IP spoofed to that of target machine. The proxy machines responds to the spoofed IP (the machine that is under attack) with the unsolicited responses.

4.	**FRAGGLE attack**: It is same as SMURF except that the hacker uses UDP echo packets instead of ICMP echo packet.

5.	**Ping flooding attack**: This is a very simple denial of service attack, where the attacking machine simply sends a massive number of ICMP (Internet Control Message Protocol) ping requests to the target machine. This attack is more effective when the attacking machine has a higher bandwidth than the target machine and has the ability to saturate the target machine's incoming bandwidth with ICMP requests. In case the target machine responds with ICMP Echo replies, the attack consumes outgoing bandwidth as well.

6.	**UDP flooding attack**: A machine experiences UDP flooding attack when the attacker sends a huge number of UDP packets to consume its resources. UDP is a connectionless protocol and as such doesn't require connection to be setup between source and destination machines to transfer data. The attacker sends the UDP packets to the IP address and a random port of target machine. The target machine, upon receiving the UDP packet, will determine what application is waiting on the port. However, as the target machine determines that there is nothing waiting, it replies with a "port unreachable" message to the sending machine. Most often, the attacker spoofs the reply address (changes it to mask the real address). The target machine crashes in case the attacker floods the target machine with enough UDP packets.

WikiLeaks

WikiLeaks is an international non-profit organization which released its website in 2006. Its purpose is to receive data via anonymous sources and leaks that would be otherwise unavailable. The confidential, secretive information then gets published on the website and becomes readily viewable by the masses. Within a year of the websites release, it has published more than 1.2 million documents. As should be evident, the site is a huge concern for the realm of knowledge security. While the website has been primarily focused on the publication of confidential information at the federal government and military level, organizational trade-secrets have also been leaked. Making matters worse is the fact that the information gets posted anonymously, so it becomes impractical for an organization to search out the individual that leaked the information and pursue litigation against him. WikiLeaks has stated its primary goal is to ensure that whistle-blowers and journalists do not receive criminal punishment such as jail-time for emailing sensitive or classified documents to the site.

For an interesting review of one of the most important cyber attack cases in recent history, review:

Ball, J. (2013, April 9). Do we need WikiLeaks any more? Retrieved from

http://www.guardian.co.uk/commentisfree/2013/apr/09/do-we-need-wikileaks

7. **BONK and Teardrop attacks**: These are old-style attacks used against old windows operating systems. The Teardrop program manipulates offset fields of a fragment in a TCP/IP packet. An offset field helps to reconstruct the defragmented packet at the destination. The machine under attack will try to reconstruct these fragmented packets but will fail because the attacker manipulates the number of packets. BONK attack is similar to Teardrop but it manipulates the fragment offset field to make a packet seem too large to reassemble. Both Bonk and Teardrop attacks cause the target machine to crash.

Key Issues in the Protection of Data

Very strong controls are required to protect sensitive information. The case of WikiLeaks getting access to confidential information was a wakeup call for all government organizations responsible for safeguarding sensitive information. IT personnel can easily protect information by instituting strong data classification controls. The organization can then start looking into the necessary level of to protect a particular piece of information. The two common data-classification approaches are military and public.

Military-based data classification is commonly used in Department of Defense and similar organizations. The military divides data into five levels:

a. Top Secret: Never disclose; damage can be grave

b. Secret: Serious damage can be caused if disclosed

c. Confidential: Damage can be caused if disclosed

d. Sensitive but unclassified: Avoid disclosure

e. Unclassified – No damage can be caused if released

Public data classification divides the data into four categories:

a. Confidential-Highest level of sensitivity and disclosure could cause serious damage to company

b. Private- Only for company use

c. Sensitive-Requires protection

d. Public-No damage caused if disclosed

Denial of service attacks are perhaps one of the major ways in which data can be lost. Some of the key characteristics are:

1. DoS attacks can be launched easily but are hard to defend. DoS attacks don't provide the attackers access to computing devices of victims, but they deny access to legitimate users. Prevention of attacks requires capital expenditure.

2. DDoS attacking tools are widely available. Years ago it required an experienced network programmer to write the code in order to attack a site. But today the tools are readily available. Though these tools may be low-tech, when combined with other similar tools, they can generate substantial traffic to pull the site off. These low-end tools don't often hide the source IP details. Thus, it is easy for a system administrator to tackle traffic.

3. Basic controls to mitigate and protect DDoS attacks are needed. Controls such as filtering can reduce the impact of DDoS attacks and reveal the attacker's identity. Filtering allows the source and destination IP of firewalls and routers to be examined. Filtering follows simple rules that delete any incoming packet that has IP in the same range as an individual's machine IP. Similarly, any outgoing traffic that doesn't have the same Source IP as an individual's machine should be deleted. The reason is that many worms, Trojans and DDoS tools forge the IP addresses.

4. Knowledgeable individuals may be capable of launching attacks by themselves without compromising third-party computers to act as zombies or recruiting a group of volunteers.

Viruses

In it's simplest form a computer virus is a computer code that successfully attaches itself to other programs and transmits itself through the network. When the infected program is launched, the viral program infests and attaches itself to other programs. The propagation occurs without the consent of the host computer or an individual.

Most viruses need some human assistance in propagating – email and downloads, shared directories, USB flash drives. A related breed of viruses is the worm. Worms typically do not attach themselves to existing computer programs, but exist independently as stand alone entities. The best way to protect computer systems from viruses is to follow some good housekeeping practice. Adherence to the following three best practices would help prevent propagation of viruses (see Kleinberg, 2007 for details):

1. Use a virus scanning/prevention software. Use of any antivirus software will help with early detection, though it may not guarantee complete prevention.

2. The least privilege principle. For instance avoid using computer with administrative rights enabled.

3. Maintain updates. Ensure that your software is patched and up to date with respect to the patches.

Useful resources

For "Models of Viral Propagation" visit: http://www.symantec.com/connect/articles/models-viral-propagation

For "How to avoid malware infections"

http://youtu.be/XL2_NaRkpLw

Attack Mitigation

There are as many ways to perpetrate a denial of service attacks, as there are people willing to try their hand at this nefarious enterprise. The tools are simple. At its most basic level, programming language C can develop routines that can have far reaching effects across the web. These C programs can use relatively benign commands that are native to the operating system (like the ping command, which is used to test the connectivity of one computer to another) or send requests to a known IP address at a specific port, and fill up the connection table of a server).

Additionally, there are real packaged applications that are available on the web to perpetrate these attacks. Some even have graphical user interfaces. Since the tools are easily available or readily written, it is important to adopt certain preventive techniques.

Defense against a DoS or DDoS attack requires several steps. First, proactive measures with strict adherence to some fundamental security policies and procedures can mitigate the exposure to an attack. Systems kept at the peak of vendor-supplied patches stay ahead of reported security breaches. Network teams should monitor the systems to determine if there have been any intrusions. A simple defensive networking mechanism is to check the incoming traffic. The router checks the incoming packets for the source IP address; if it is not a valid address, router drops the packet.

Second, one needs to know the symptoms in order to determine if the system is indeed under attack. A site may experience a spike in regular traffic if it becomes really popular. These are normal occurrences. However, there are certain indictors of probable attack. For example, programs may run very slowly, there is a high failure rates for HTTP services, a large number of connection requests arrive from various networks, users complain about slow or no site access, or the machine may show an unexplained very high CPU load.

So, now you are under attack. What can you do to mitigate the damage? You might like to trace the attacking packets back to their origin; however, it will be of little help if the source IP address is spoofed so you can't get to the real source. Alternatively, you can trace the originating router and back track the traffic from router to router. Once the traffic is backtracked to the source, you might put a filter in place to block the traffic. This will be a time consuming effort. Moreover, by determining the type of traffic that is being used for the attack, you can limit the of rate traffic. This will restrict the bandwidth provided to the specific type of traffic. A more drastic solution is **black hole filtering,** where an ISP can send the offending traffic to a null location, for example, to the /dev/null file on a UNIX system

In summary, the three basic techniques to prevent DDoS attacks are: 1) **Bandwidth**- While providing large amount of bandwidth circumvent the probable attacks, there is always a limitation on the amount of resources allocated. Once the attacker can reach that level by generating meaningless traffic, DDoS is experienced, which turns out the legitimate users. 2) **Traceback** - Traceback traces the packets back to the originating source. Once the source IP is known, ISP can configure the router to reject the packets originating from that particular IP. The router sends the ICMP (Internet Control Message Protocol) type 3- destination unreachable messages back to the source machine. 3) **Mitigation**- Mitigation offered by vendors like VeriSign and Symantec uses traffic cleaning center operating at peering points on the internet. The nodes scrub the traffic directing only clean traffic to web servers.

Issues and Concerns

Without a prepared and effective information security plan, organizations face some important challenges when dealing with distributed computing and knowledge security, including:

- Costs and risks associated with data leaking
- Determining responsible parties and individuals in a distributed, dynamic computing environment
- Creating a security culture which fosters employee accountability and liability
- Ongoing, recurring costs of managing external identities

As we have begun to discuss, there are many issues that occur when trying to apply information security principles in a distributed environment. One such problem is the fact that human beings are the main proponents of these systems. Therefore, a strong dependence is placed on people's behavior. We assume that employees will make ethical decisions and not attempt circumventing security procedures in place. They also need to be trusted to properly use the data they access and help safeguard it. This is an important characteristic of an organization. We must be willing to trust our employees, but humans have flaws and we must find adequate ways of deciding how to trust each other. Determining appropriate ways for gaining trust is paramount for an organization to maintain security.

With regards to cloud computing, data visibility must also be considered. If we remember how cloud computing works, in regards to systems being loaned out to companies, an organization should thusly determine how their data will be stored in the cloud. From a physical storage perspective, the data is usually located in a shared environment with other companies' data alongside it. Assurance must be met that data will be properly segregated from that of another organization. Efforts must be met to guarantee that only trusted individuals will be able to access the data. Furthermore, the data must be stored securely when at rest and it must be able to move securely from one location to another.

Another concern for distributed computing environments comes about when a data breach were to actually occur, who is to be held responsible? If we think back to the old mainframe systems that were centrally located in a server room, there were only a few select individuals that had access to the system. Additionally, there was usually only one individual assigned to be responsible for the system – which, again, contained almost all of the company's data on that single system. Therefore, if a security breach were to ever take place, the specific individual would be held responsible for not properly protecting the system. Direct judgment and punishment could then be applied against him. Yet as we move to a distributed environment where data resides in many places, it becomes much more difficult for determining who is to be held accountable for the data and systems that they reside on. In a distributed environment, there is a much larger user base than before. It can be very overbearing for one individual to manage.

Developing a security culture within an organization is vital to get employees to protect data and individually perform a role related to the security of their knowledge and data. Security policies can be enacted to establish the guidelines and procedures for employees to follow when accessing data, but a vital concern is around getting users to follow the policies that have been placed in effect. Without a security culture in place, no one will invest in security activities if it does not benefit them. As an example, if only a few employees were to embrace the security policies and everyone else ignores them, the company is not safe. There are still numerous potential holes in the organization that an attacker can easily exploit. Naturally, it holds that as more employees embrace the policies, there are fewer holes. For a policy to become effective, all employees must embrace it.

When referring to distributed computing, collaboration and the sharing of information can span several domains, each one having its own administration and access control policy. Controls need to be set in place when multiple organizations work together so that individual compliance requirements and policies will be fulfilled by all parties. Over the past several years, business and legal requirements have been able to be implemented through simplified, technical solutions, allowing enterprises to achieve unprecedented levels of collaboration. As the collaboration between enterprise domains increase, we also begin to find issues around the management of external users. Companies now provide core business applications that require trusted access for people that are not company employees.

Current Methods of Protection

Current methods of protecting distributed computing environments and knowledge security include, but are not limited to:

- Establishing trust in employees, computers, and resources
- Creating a security policy and fostering a security culture
- Protecting data through encryption and data classification

In distributed computing environments, it is often necessary to establish trust before entities interact together. The process of trusting warm-bodies (employees) can often become an elaborate and daunting task for organizations when not properly executed. It is especially challenging as a simple technical solution cannot be applied to the problem of determining if a person is trustworthy or not. There are steps an organization can take to better understand how trustworthy a person is (such as using background checks to see if they lied on their employment application, were ever arrested, or are heavily in debt and may be "persuaded" by a competitor to steal sensitive information). Ultimately, however, placing trust in an individual is a game of chance. It should also be noted that performing a background check on a potential job applicant before hiring them is not a helpful tool if future check-ins on an employee's status are not conducted. This is an important step that many organizations still do not take to this day.

Placing trust in computers and resources can be just as difficult as trusting employees, yet many solutions are available. In a distributed environment, it is very common for internal users to access external systems outside of an organization's domain of control, and for external users to access internal systems. This creates a fundamental problem in which the domain of control for these resources and identities are outside of the organization's scope. Identity federation provides a solution to this issue through the use of open industry standards and specifications. The ultimate goal of federation is to enable users of one domain to securely and effortlessly access data from another domain without the need for redundant user administration. A federated environment enables business partners to achieve integration by providing a mechanism for companies to share identity information across their respective security domains.

When utilizing cloud technology, trusting cloud providers and how they will handle your data are important concerns for an organization. Companies must demand transparency from vendors, avoiding parties that refuse to provide detailed information on their security programs and procedures. Questions should be asked which provide insight into the qualifications of vendor's policy makers, architects, programmers and operators; vendor applicable risk-control processes and technical mechanisms; and to ensure that vendors can identify unanticipated vulnerabilities. Inquiries should also be made looking into the vendor's security policies and ensuring that they provide adequate coverage while meeting the organization's compliance requirements mandated by state and federal laws.

Almost every organization has a security policy created and used throughout their environment, but this does not necessarily equate to a security culture. Having a policy in writing and ensuring that all employees comply with it are two entirely different things. For a policy to become effective, all employees must embrace it. Understanding how to get an individual to comply with the policies in place can be a difficult and complex task. Disciplinary actions can be prescribed against individuals that do not comply with the set policies (either because of laziness, ignorance, or malevolence). Yet the problem of using disciplinary actions against uncooperative employees is that it is a corrective action in nature. It will not prevent a security breach from occurring, but will instead only aid in the finger-pointing that will occur afterwards.

A new approach must be used to look at how to get individuals to comply with the existing security policy. The bootstrap problem is a concept which states that employees will only notice the benefits of policy adoption after a certain number of users exist that already comply with the policies. Another way of looking at this concept is everyone simply joining the bandwagon; once a certain percentage of employees adopt the policies, everyone else will hopefully fall in line. Education, awareness, and training are aimed at this bootstrapping problem by helping employees understand the benefits that such policies can create. Most importantly is gaining executive support and buy-in for any policy to be quickly adopted. Executives must actively lead the change by altering their own behaviors and provide value in the significance of the policy adoption.

From a technical perspective, with data flowing in many different directions in a distributed environment, encryption of the data is vital -- both when the data is at-rest and when it is moving across a communication medium. As the data can ultimately end up on hundreds of servers and computers, it can be difficult to effectively manage. Encryption is an effective tool as it provides an extremely high degree of protection. If encrypted data were to be stolen or leaked, it is useless without the means to decipher it. Generally speaking, adding security to a system often narrows its usability. Yet the most successful data encryption solutions enable a business to flow at a normal pace. They silently secure the data in the background, while the normal end-user is unaware and unaffected by its use.

Another means of protecting data in a distributed environment is through the process of classifying it. Data classification is the process used to assign a level of sensitivity to data as it is being created, modified, stored, or transmitted. The classification of data is used to determine the extent to which the data needs to be controlled. Proper classification helps place applicable controls around the data. This is essential if you are to differentiate between data that is of little (or any) value, and data which is highly sensitive and confidential. The varying levels of control not only help apply technical processes around the access of this data, but also help define for employees which data can absolutely not be shared with others and that which is of little concern. Furthermore, by properly classifying data, its encryption becomes simplified as only the more sensitive data needs to be encrypted. By not encrypting public data, valuable computational time and hard drive space related to the actual encryption process is saved.

In a distributed environment where data cannot be centrally managed, assigning agents to oversee the flow of specific sets of data helps to provide a degree of administration over the data. Business roles are often given to individuals to facilitate in the classification and protection of the organization's data. An individual must exist with the authority to control access to the data and to make the difficult decisions related to how it is to be used and protected. The data owner is the one who makes these decisions. This person needs to be carefully chosen as he/she needs to actually understand the sensitivity of the data and its importance within the company. Another important role is a data custodian. This individual helps protect the data as they are the one who controls the physical access to the data. She also monitors how the data is accessed and reports any discrepancies and risks back to the data owner, who will then take various corrective actions. This position is typically filled by system administrators and those that manage the servers and storage devices. Finally, user managers are assigned and given the responsibility of enrolling users in having access to the data and vouching for their identities. Additional responsibilities may include supervising the use of data by users and instructing them with how they can further assist in the protection of the data.

Evolution of Protection ████████████████████

Discussed up to this point have been mechanisms that many companies already take to mitigate distributed computing and knowledge security concerns. A few solutions exist that only a smaller percentage of organizations have moved towards. These solutions include:

- moving large, organizational structures to smaller, manageable units

- determining how to transition employee motivations from altruistic to extrinsic reasons

- reevaluating security policies and adding effective preventative measures

Most organizations today follow a hierarchical business model with its CEO at the top of the tree and people branch off of him. As this organizational structure may work in many organizations, the culture of information processing is evolving with more data reaching an ever-increasing number of people; causing the data to be difficult to manage. Hierarchical structures may need to be reevaluated to find a system where people can quickly and easily access and send out data in a more free-flowing environment. This would also allow for the control of this data to be pushed out to operational units, where the actual transactions on the data occur.

To illustrate this, in a sample distributed environment, an essential resource for distributed computing such as Telecommunications would be controlled by multiple departments. By using a hierarchical organizational model, it would cause a push-pull force between departments: network administrators (who feel they should control all telecommunications as it is part of their job descriptions) and information security specialists (who feel that all telecommunication activity is a security issue and needs to be managed by their department). As is shown, complexity often arises in trying to centrally manage the operation and security of systems in a hierarchical model. To combat this concern, many CIOs have started to push more of this power to individual users. Additional middle-management structures are then created who can better manage this power-sharing with users while maintaining data and application integrity.

In 1999, James Odell and David Greenstein presented a white paper addressing the fact that organizations moving towards distributed computing should consider changing their organizational structures. They argued that large, centralized IT organizations need to be broken down into simpler, smaller business units that are each individually responsible for their own business, financial, and production success. They compared their recommendation of business units to the cells of an organism. These smaller, distributed organizational cells would allow units to quickly reorganize and react to threats and changing market conditions. The transition would better align with the goal of breeding cooperation among departments, instead of focusing on power, authority, and how to get the largest percentage of the IT budget.

This would allow the protection of distributed computing and knowledge security to be easily broken down to the management of data at the individual unit's necessity to access it. It reduces the potential of another unit's data being accidentally accessed. Units can have their own servers and resources where another unit does not have access to it unless explicitly given. A flatter organization allows executives that used to have no clue about the issues and risks that were really occurring at the endpoints of the organization to have a much stronger grasp of the issues causing security vulnerabilities. Furthermore, just like evolution and the adage provided by Charles Darwin regarding survival of the fittest, if an organizational unit (or cell) fails to effectively contribute to the organization, other areas do not fail and the flawed unit simply dies.

Another common approach to organizational modeling is distributed security. With this concept, the entire IT organization isn't broken down into smaller units – just the information security department. In this model, there is a central security team that performs the normal daily security functions such as risk assessment, identity management, and security architecture. However, the emphasis is placed on enabling more individuals outside of security to act as delegated security administrators. These individuals act as proponents of information security practices, making sure that the specific teams and units that these individuals work on are following security practices. Common responsibilities also include educating peers and reporting back to the central security department upon the discovery of issues or concerns. This model essentially ensures that security is added to every link of the organizational chain, instead of only existing as a small group within the enterprise that fully comprehend and manage the security risks and vulnerabilities.

An important part of creating a security culture where humans interact in an ethical manner, protecting data and keeping knowledge safe, is to better understand what motivates and influences individuals. Current practices within an organization dictate to simply discipline an employee if they do not follow enacted policies and procedures. Unfortunately, this process uses negative feedback for when these standards are not followed, instead of providing positive feedback when they are properly followed. The use of fear for motivational purposes may be a useful tool, but it is arguably not the most effective one on the grounds that there is no obvious and direct return on investment for an individual if he behaves in a secure manner. Organizations need to foster an environment where employees choose the interest of the company over their own self-interest. Using positive incentives as a replacement for negative ones might make sense in Information Security management.

Case in point, it may be common for members of a programming team to share passwords or avoid writing detailed documentation in order to quickly wrap up an assignment and meet a necessary deadline. In the short term, these practices might be beneficial to the organization. Yet over time, these habits can cause considerable damages, both monetarily and legally. Giving positive feedback to employees who behave in an especially secure manner can be extremely motivating for them. This does not only create an organization that is secure, but one that is rewarding for employees to work for as well. Positive feedback breeds an open and supportive culture causing an elevated level of trust to be built within the organization.

Employees who possess the ability to distinguish and report on questionable ethical issues are a significant asset to a company. These individuals help prevent possible security issues before they can occur by recognizing behavioral and attitude shifts in coworkers. Such changes in attitude may lead to a revengeful or apathetic mindset, resulting in a security breach or data leak. This concept of ethical awareness is an essential area of knowledge security as technical solutions cannot be easily applied to secure the knowledge that people possess in their heads. We are forced to rely on their trustworthiness, constantly monitoring their actions for flags that might allude to a change in their dependability. To do so, we occasionally need to look beyond first appearances. Ethical issues are not always so easy to spot. In fact, sometimes, they may start out looking like something else entirely.

For instance, assume that an ambitious young manager's performance suddenly starts to deteriorate. Normally, this would hardly be considered an ethical issue, until we begin to consider the sudden and unprovoked change in attitude. One possibility could be that the young man has just become heavily in debt from a financial perspective. Poor work performance can sometimes also mean a lack of interest in the duties that an individual performs. And, while it is definitely a stretch, it could mean that the manager is thinking about leaving the company soon. More often than not, the most likely time for an employee to steal company information is when they are about to leave an organization. The stolen information may not involve company trade secrets or social security numbers. Nevertheless, an individual may find it beneficial to take a copy of a recent architectural document she had just completed as it could prove to be beneficial at her new job, saving her some unnecessary time of duplicating a great deal of information she had already worked on. As this case shows, the organization's security culture needs to have employees look beyond what they see at first glance. Unethical behavior is not always so obvious. If an employee observes or suspects questionable actions by another, they should discuss it with the person affected, bring it to the attention of leadership, or make an Integrity Helpline report.

Additionally, more organizations need to foster an Open Door Policy allowing employees to feel both comfortable and respected for raising possible security and ethical concerns. While methods of motivating employees to report issues have already been discussed, there is still a necessity to develop a way in which employees can anonymously report a concern. One such method is the creation of an Integrity Helpline. As there is a fine line between business relationships and personal relationships created at work, employees can sometimes become aware of questionable actions that another employee may engage in through their friendships. Willingness to escalate a security concern and possibly ruin a friendship is something that businesses need to be willing to battle with. One step towards making this decision a little easier for employees is to at least allow them to raise an issue in a secure and anonymous manner. At a minimum, this will help alleviate some employee concerns around being singled-out by their peers.

Conclusion

Many companies that choose to move towards distributed environments often do so to save money. Yet, as has been shown, this migration also comes with an increase in the risks and issues that can result from business data moving across many different forms of media. Over time, these additional risks become overbearing for companies and a strong need emerges to move back to a centralized, mainframe model. This cycle often repeats in organizations as the lack of funds causes a move towards decentralization and the resulting complexities and risks cause a migration back towards the centralization of resources. It is a natural business practice that occurs as newer technologies and processes emerge. Key decision makers use the distributed computing approach as a contingency plan while they grow support and the necessary funding to eventually develop the proper centralized approach.

Numerous organizations have also managed to create a sustainable distributed environment over time, yet the necessary time and funds to create such a well-thought out environment is often higher than originally anticipated. Knowledgeable and experienced individuals that can develop such a cooperative, secure distributed environment exist but often come at a very high cost to companies. Management must be willing to spend the necessary time to adequately determine the correct approach for their organizations while further considering the risks and resources involved.

Managing knowledge can be just as difficult. It is impossible to track ideas and information as they flow through a company by word of mouth. Employees can easily share passwords with each and leak confidential information to competitors. Hiring and maintaining trustworthy individuals is fundamental to the success of knowledge security. By creating a unified security culture, assurance can be met by a much higher degree that employees feel responsible for the overall protection of the company. Technical solutions can help solve many security issues, but the best form of protecting knowledge is in the form of the human element. The process of empowering individuals to take action when they notice the occurrence of unethical behavior simply adds an additional layer of defense to any security program.[2]

---

[2] Many thanks to my student Christopher Bell for his contributions to this chapter.

Four

4. Cyber Espionage

The Basics ████████████████████

What is industrial espionage? Simply put, industrial espionage is obtaining **trade secrets** by **dishonest means**. The trade secrets could be in the form of research data, blueprints, business or national plans. Dishonest means could range from telephone or computer tapping, infiltration of competitor workforce, eavesdropping, among others. There are two classes of Industrial Espionage that need to be considered, **corporate spying** and **state-sponsored spying**.

Corporate spying is typically confined to theft of business secrets, including patent wars. In 2013, Merck Pharmaceutical's Indian subsidiary dragged a domestic generic drug manufacturer, Glenmark, to court for producing a more affordable version of the diabetes drug, Junuvia. In another 2013 case, a California District Court ruled that Mattel, Inc. had indeed engaged in corporate spying against the maker of Bratz dolls. Over the years there have been several corporate espionage cases. There were several notable cases. One was *Cadence Design Systems v. Avant!* (2002), where Avant! allegedly stole code from Cadence. In another case, in 1982, IBM sued Hitachi when Hitachi mysteriously had possession of IBM's Adirondack Workbook, a set of computer specifications and planning memos. The list goes on. However most corporate spying cases relate to seeking competitive edge over a rival.

See most notorious acts of corporate espionage here:

Business Pundit. (2011, April 25). 10 Most Notorious Acts of Corporate Espionage.   Retrieved from http://www.businesspundit.com/10-most-notorious-acts-of-corporate-espionage/

Watch corporate espionage state of affairs:

Vanderburg, E. (2012, November 2). Corporate espionage on the rise in Northeast Ohio [video]. Retrieved from

http://youtu.be/75Pz9TDQ-2g

In recent years **state-sponsored spying** has received significant attention. In February 2013 *Wall Street Journal*, *New York Times* and *Washington Post* disclosed that their computer systems had been compromised. Blame was attributed on cyber espionage from China. The US Secretary of State acknowledged the magnitude of the problem, as did the Defense Secretary who termed it as a "cyber Pearl Harbor" (Panetta, 2012).

It is not just the US that has seen a barrage of cyber espionage attacks. In the UK, the **Center for Protection of National Infrastructure** recently issued a warning that parts of UK's critical infrastructure are under attack through an ongoing series of "email-borne" electronic attacks (CPNI, 2005). Canada has issued similar warnings.

Fascinating read about Chinese cyber espionage:

Healey, J. (2013, February 21). Fighting Chinese Cyberespionage: Obama's Next Move. US News and World Report. Retrieved from http://www.usnews.com/opinion/blogs/world-report/2013/02/21/fighting-chinese-cyberespionage-obamas-next--move

Evidence that the Chinese Army is behind cyber attacks:

CNN. (2013, February 19). China is sponsoring cyber-espionage [video]. Retrieved fromhttp://youtu.be/1dxH53zJt5o

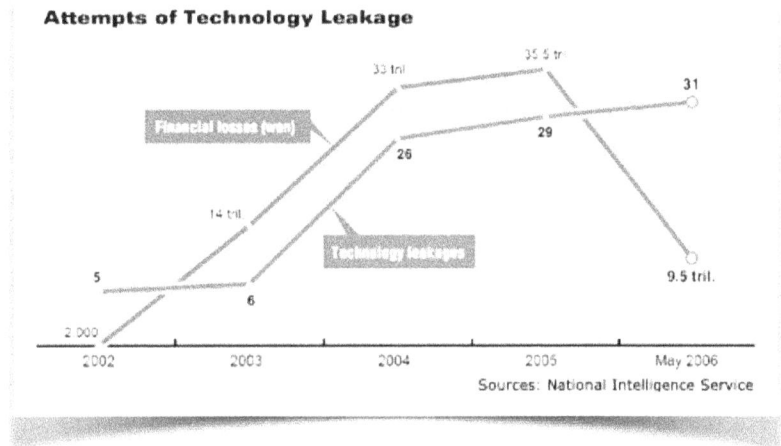

Figure 4.1, Attempts of technology leakage (see Korea Times article at: http://large.stanford.edu/history/kaist/references/china/kim/)

An interesting issue came to light following the disappearance of the Malaysian flight MH370. It has been reported that a modified version of the hacker tool, Poison Ivy, was used through a group "Admin@338". Poison Ivy is one of the favorite tools in Chinese State Sponsored attacks. The attacks began two days after the disappearance of the flight and specifically targeted a South East Asian country. A US based think tank was also targeted. The reasons for the attacks could have been many, however reports suggest that they were specifically targeted to gather international trade, finance and economic policy data. The cost of espionage is significant. According to a report published in *Epoch Times*, "The FBI estimates that economic espionage costs the U.S. $13 billion a year, yet their numbers are based only on current FBI cases where spies have been caught and charged. It does not include the majority of theft that was not reported, or the scale of breaches that are unknown to the companies."[3]

Information Brokerage

Cyber security problems related to **information brokerage** affects both private companies and nation states. While the business of brokering information is legal, technical, formal and normative controls are quite ill defined. The business of information brokerage relates to individuals or businesses searching on behalf of the clients. Traditionally, information brokers were library scientists who would work on behalf of authors and research companies to search data and catalogue it. However, over the years the business has grown in scope and complexity.

In recent years, two particular breaches came to the fore – those of Choice Point and Reed Elsevier (parent of LexusNexis). Both companies were accused of invading the privacy of millions of motorists in Florida. Both companies had collected sensitive personal data and had resold it. In 2006, Choice point was also in the middle of a controversy when hackers had stolen identity of nearly 300,000 Californians from Choice Point systems.

In 2012, the Federal Trade Commission began investigating nine information brokerage firms (Acxiom, Corelogic, Datalogix, eBureau, ID Analytics, Intelius, Peekyou, Rapleaf, and Recorded Future) for their practices in data collection and use. Typically data brokers do not interact directly with the consumer, but collect information from public records, correlate data and resell it to other businesses. Since all this happens without the consent of a consumer, there is sharp criticism of information

---

[3] http://www.theepochtimes.com/n3/326002-the-staggering-cost-of-economic-espionage-against-the-us/

brokers making money by repackaging information that belongs to someone else. This is indeed a very special case of **Consumer Espionage**.

In a rather interesting article, Dhillon & Chapman (2006) discuss the case of DoubleClick, which had traditionally been in the business of banner advertising on the Internet. They then acquired Abacus Direct, merged the databases and began tracking user online clicks and their physical location. While the information was of great marketing value, it was certainly on the boundaries of ethical use. At the time of the merger of DoubleClick and Abacus, the Federal Trade Commission (FTC) did not seem to have any privacy concerns, until later, when the consumer groups began complaining, the FTC stepped up their investigations.

Government documents worth reading about cyber espionage

H.R. Rep. 1707, 112th Cong., 1st Sess. 7 (2011). Retrieved from

http://www.govtrack.us/congress/bills/112/hr1707

For FTC guidelines visit:

FTC. (2012, March). Protecting Consumer Privacy in an Era of Rapid Change: Recommendations for Businesses and Policymakers. Federal Trade Commission.

Retrieved from http://ftc.gov/os/2012/03/120326privacyreport.pdf

---

The intentions of most information brokers are genuine. However, there are cases where the knowledge of the processes and of the industry have been used for personal gain. There was an interesting case that surfaced several years ago, with mounting evidence of illegal information brokering in the oil industry. In the late 1990s, a list of some 50 suspect individuals was drawn by the UK-based Serious Fraud Office to investigate North Sea oil purchasing. One of the early cases to be prosecuted was that of Jozef Szrajber, who in 1984 was found selling confidential British Petroleum information. Five years later Szrajber was caught while trying to bribe an Esso employee. Investigations in UK and Norway found that JSzrajber had employed another agent, Paolo Sorelli, an Italian engineering parts trader (see Beckman, 1997 for details on this particular case).

Regulatory controls around information brokers are virtually non-existent. In the UK, illegal information brokering has not been defined as an offense, only a conspiracy to fraud with a maximum sentence of 3 years. In the US a bill was passed through in the 111th Congress and later revived in the 112th Congress as H.R. 1707. The bill contains several requirements for auditing information brokers and has particular reference to transparency of practices. While the bill was introduced, it has not been enacted. In 2012, the Federal Trade Commission issued guidelines advising businesses about privacy, data and security. Such guidelines are usually advisory in nature and do not necessarily ensure censure.

Watch the following video. It is about spying and espionage prevention. Although it is an old view from the DoD, it certainly bring home the point.

Dept. of Defense. (1965). Unauthorized Disclosure [video]. Retrieved from http://youtu.be/vUJhDYml1ns

This is another video that related to economic espionage.

CPNI UK. (2012, November 29). Piece of cake [video]. Retrieved from http://youtu.be/kunc5EeN7Dk

---

Intelligence Gathering or Espionage

There is a fine line between what can be considered intelligence gathering and what would be termed espionage. Crane (2005) suggest three criteria that could determine if indeed there was an ethical problem with the manner in which information was gathered:

- The tactic relates to the manner in which information was collected. It might just be that the process was not deemed acceptable.

- The nature of information sought is also an important consideration. Some basic questions need to be asked – Was the information private and confidential? Was it publicly available?

• The purpose for which the information was collected. The following questions need consideration – How is the information going to be used? Is someone going to monetize it? Would it be used against public interest?

Tactics for gathering intelligent information takes several forms. Whatever be the kind of a tactic used, the origins are usually dubious and ethicality questionable. Most tactics are in violation of the philosopher Immanuel Kant's categorical imperative – only those actions are acceptable, which can be universalized. Most tactics are clearly illegal and unethical. These might range from breaking into competitors' offices and computer systems to wire tapping, hiring private detectives and going thorough competitors' trash to find confidential information.

Top ways in which corporate spies steal information

Contact is established with secretaries and office assistants in informal settings

Individuals are tricked into filling surveys to collect information

Spies may call local hotels to find the schedule for corporate events

Accounts may be set up with job sites where the company may be advertising so as to send fake resumes and gather company information or even engage in fake head hunter schemes

Spies may act as fake journalists to interview key individuals and tour the premises

Spies may engage in "dumpster dives" to go through the trash

Spies have an extraordinary ability to snoop in on conversations

(Source: Javers, E. (2010). *Broker, Trader, Lawyer, Spy: The secret world of corporate espionage.* New York: Harper-Collins.)

The Nature of Information brings to bear the question, what constitutes private or public information? There is no doubt that companies have the right to keep their private information confidential. However, one may argue that the information belongs to individuals not corporations. This raises an interesting dilemma – what is the boundary of a corporation? A corporation is, after all, a collection of individuals. This means that the property rights needs to be clarified.

Cyber espionage motivation ████████████

The reason information is collected is intricately linked to aspects of public interest. Of particular concern are cases where corporate intelligence related to national and international security is obtained. In such cases several public interest issues come to the fore. See figure 4.2 to see how cyber espionage is undertaken. Some examples include:

- Anticompetitive behaviors, including deliberate removal of competitors
- Price hikes
- Entrenchment of monopoly position

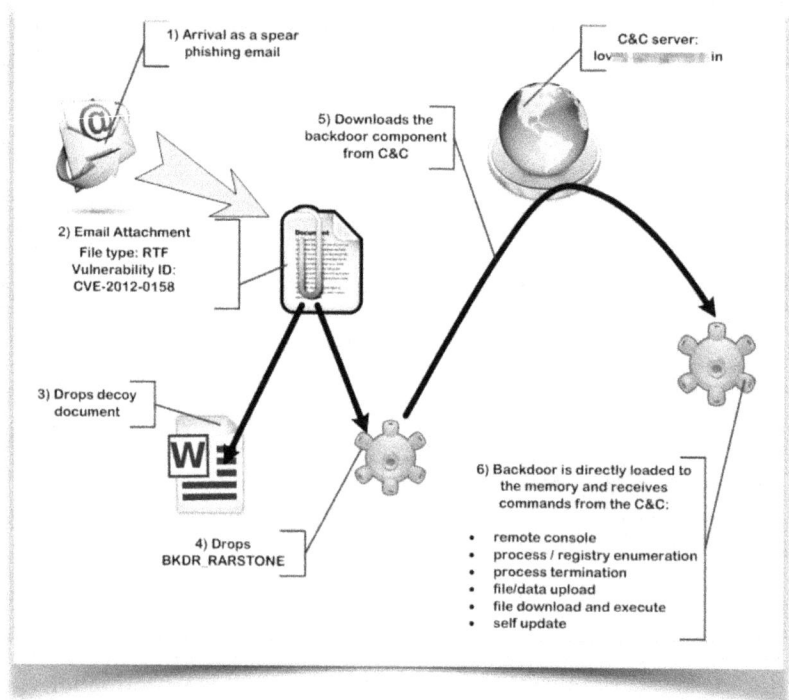

Figure 4.2. Cyber espionage process

An example – the case of Shell Nigeria

Following the WikiLeaks debacle, it came to light that Shell Petroleum executives had infiltrated the Nigerian government.

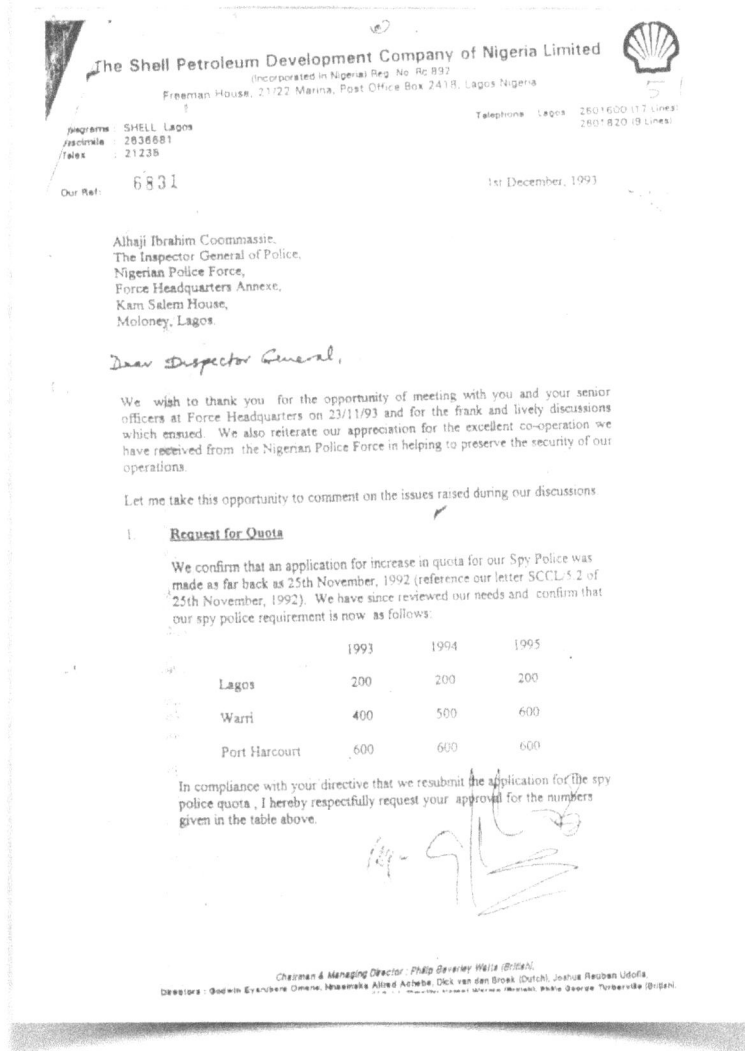

Figure 4.3 Shell documentation.

(Source: http://goo.gl/6iE8Vu)

Shell released a 1993 letter from Philip Watts, Chairman and Managing Director of Shell (Nigeria). Watts made a specific request to increase the number of spies to 1400 individuals.

Spyware and Espionage

One of the weapons of choice in the 21ˢᵗ century espionage is the Botnet. What required the resources of a nation state in the 1970s and 80s can now be accomplished by tech savvy users located anywhere in the world. A term that is often used is that of "web robots" since these are programs that tend to take over the infected computer. In that sense a "bot" is a malware. And since a network of computers are usually involved, hence the term "botnets". "Zombies" is also a term that is often used to describe botnets. This is because typically an infected computer *bids for the master*. Following an infestation by a Bot can enable the following kinds of acts (more details can be found in Schiller and Binkley, 2011):

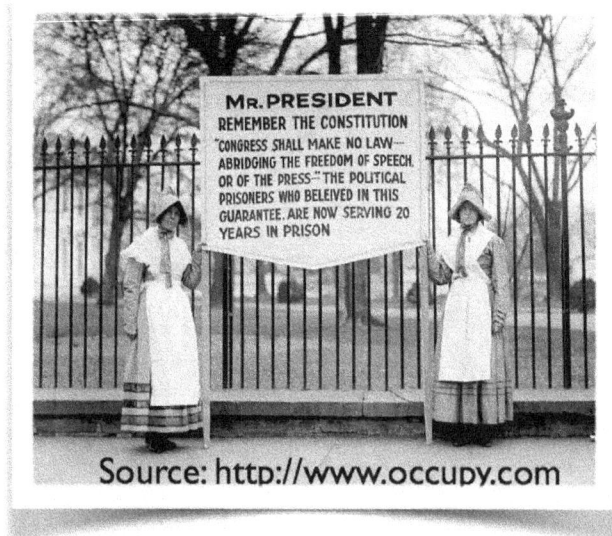

Figure 4.4, Protecting whistleblowers. Originally published in Truthout

Sending: The computer can send spam, viruses and spyware

Stealing: Personal and private information can be stolen and sent back to the malicious user. Such information could include credit card numbers, bank credentials and other sensitive information

Denial of Service: Cybercriminals can resort to demanding ransom or a range of other criminal acts.

Click fraud: Bots are used to increase web-advertising billings. This is accomplished by automatic clicking on URLs and online advertisements.

Summary

This chapter explored the types of industrial espionage. It examined corporate spying and state-sponsored spying, and how the brokerage of information by employees affects both private companies and nation states. Next, the module took a look at the issues which separate corporate espionage and legitimate intelligence gathering. Finally, you reviewed the motivations for cyber espionage.

5. Cryptography

The Basics

It was perhaps until the 1970s that the National Security Agency practically had a monopoly on encryption technologies. The change came with the publication of an article by professors, Whitfield Diffie and Martin Hellman, from Stanford University, New Directions in Cryptography". The publication of this article changed the landscape completely. Cryptography as a field god established and to undertake research in this field became fashionable. One might ask how the article by Diffie and Hellman changed the field. Well, they proposed what come to be known as *public-key cryptosystems*. The public-key algorithm proposed by the authors came to be known as the Diffie-Hellman algorithm. A competing conceptualization was later proposed by Massachusetts institute of Technology computer scientists – Roland Rivest, Adi Shamir and Leonard Adleman (RSA).

Encryption ██████████████████████████

Encryption is based on the science of cryptography, which has been in existence ever since the advent of the human race. The Greek Spartan generals were known to receive sensitive messages in a thin wooden cylinder called a **scytale.** The message would be written on a piece of parchment around the length of the scytale. The message would be gibberish without a corresponding scytale. The parchment had to be wrapped around it for the message to be read.

The Greeks were also among the first to use ciphers, particularly involving substitution and transposition. Once of the earliest ciphers was named by Julius Caesar as well – the Caesar Cipher. Modern day cryptography however relies extensively on computers. This is because human based code is rather easy to break.

Figure 5.1, Images of a scytale cipher

For more Information, please explore the following resources:

Download the Caesar Cipher from here:

Secret Code Breaker. (n.d.). Caesar Cipher. Secret Code Breaker. Online Cryptanalyst's Handbook. Retrieved from:

http://www.secretcodebreaker.com/caesar-cipher.html

Learn more about the Caesar Cipher here:

Khan Academy. (2012). The Caesar Cipher. Ancient Cryptography. Retrieved from

http://www.khanacademy.org/math/applied-math/cryptography/crypt/v/caesar-cipher

How Cryptography Works

Modern day cryptography has two types of encryption systems – *Symmetric Key* and *Public Key* encryption.

Symmetric Key encryption requires the each of the communicating computers to have a secret key. The secret code is used to encrypt the information prior to it being transmitted. The code is essentially a secret code that is used to decode the information at the receiving end.

In the U.S., the Data Encryption Standard, which used a 56 bit key, was adopted in the 1970s. A 56 bit key can have over 70 quadrillion combinations. Over the years DES has been replaced by Advanced Encryption Standard, with 128, 192 and 256 bit keys.

Public Key encryption was an advancement on symmetric key encryption in that it uses two different keys – public and private, at the same time. The private key is typically known only to the sender computer and the public key is available to any receiving computer. The key pair is based on prime numbers and for this reason there is high security. The Public Key encryptions became rather popular with the invention of *Pretty Good Privacy* program (PGP).

SSL and TSL. An important development in the implementation of public key encryption is the **Secure Sockets Layer (SSL)**. SSL was an invention of Netscape and has now emerged to be a standard Internet Security Protocol, particularly for transferring web browser based sensitive information. Today SSL is part of the

Transport Layer Security, the overall security protocol. The use of SSL/TSL in a browser can be identified by the use of "https" in the URL or even a small padlock in the status bar. In most cases the use is automatic and seamless for the user.

Some Examples

In the paragraphs below some examples of cryptography are presented.

Mono-alphabetic substitution. This is perhaps one of the easiest forms of ciphers. There is a straightforward one to one mapping between the plain text and the ciphertext. In this case the key to decrypt shall always be a permutation of the 26 alphabets of the English language. For example:

```
a b c d e f g h i j k l m n o p q r s t u v w x y z

Z Y X W V U T S R Q P O N M L K J I H G F E D C B A
```

So, the message such a "come here" would be encrypted as:

XLNV SVIV

It is rather easy to break this kind of an encryption largely because the mapping of letters to cipher is fixed and there is a known probability of certain alphabets appearing together. In English language for example the letter "e" has the highest relative frequency of appearing (about 13%) and j, x, q, and z the least. In fact "z" appears only 1% of the time. In our example above, the letter "e" is enciphered as "v". This means that "v" will be the most common character in the cipher text. Advanced statistical techniques can then be used to narrow down the code breaking process.

Polybius Square. This technique is named after Polybius, a Greek historian (220-118 BC). Besides cryptography, Polybius is also credited with his pioneering ideas concerning separation of power in government. In a Polybius Square the letters of the alphabet are arranged left to right and top to bottom. In modern times I and J are usually combined to produce a 5x5 table. The table could take the following form:

Table 5.1, A Polybius Square

	1	2	3	4	5
1	A	B	C	D	E
2	F	G	H	I/J	K
3	L	M	N	O	P
4	Q	R	S	T	U
V5W	V	W	X	Y	Z

To use the Polybius square, lets consider the example "go there". The letter "g" is located at the intersection of row 2 and column 2, so the coded message would begin with number "22" (typically the row number is written before the column number. The coded message for "go there" would then be:

```
         G  O        T  H  E  R  E
        22  34       44 23 15 42 15
```

The Polybius Square is not particularly difficult to decode. However, mixing up numbers and omitting certain alphabets increases complexity and hence the ability to decode.

For more Information, please explore the following resources:

There are several other variations of the Polybius Square method. The details can be found at:

Bifid cipher. (n.d.) In Wikipedia.

Retrieved from http://en.wikipedia.org/wiki/Bifid_cipher

http://en.wikipedia.org/wiki/Trifid_cipher

The video below shows a variant of the Polybius Square

Lam, K. (2012, May 9). Playfair Cipher Explained [Video file].

Retrieved from http://youtu.be/quKhvu2tPy8

Security Plans

Security plans are fundamental for the success of any security strategy. While there are several organizational issues that need to be considered in the development and design of a security plan, central to these is the manner in which private information is kept confidential. In this module while we have explained the fundamentals of encryption and cryptography, there seems to be a flawed understanding, partially promoted by popular press. Reference to 128-keys relative to 64-bit keys seems to suggest that the 128-bit key is better than the other. The reality however is very different. A good analogy is the lock on the front door of a house. The key to the house is essentially working with the position of the leavers and the possible number of keys to work with a certain number of combinations of leavers in the lock. Sooner or later a burglar will be able to crack the lock. However the question that arises is, what is the best possible way to break into the house? It is simpler and easier to break the door or a window, disguise as someone else or simply rob a key at gunpoint.

Thus, when designing security of enterprises, an exclusive reliance on cryptographic methods should be discouraged and reviewed in light of the overall security of the enterprise. There are at least three considerations that security planners need to address.

1. **Cryptographic designs**. A good analogy to understand cryptographic designs is that of architecture and physical buildings. It is certainly possible to build a building with the best of the materials, but it may still not be the best design because of the manner in which the materials may have been put together. Many a times buildings collapse not because of bad materials, but because of bad designs. Similarly a cryptographic system is a function of several elements - encryption algorithms, digital signatures, hash functions, message authentications. Security can be compromised if any of the building blocks of a cryptographic design get compromised. Assuring quality of the overall design therefore is critical to the success of any security plan.

2. **Implementation**. Many of the security plans fail because of bad implementation. At times the plaintext just sits on the drive or the virtual memory of the machine. This results in the complete compromise of the system. In other cases the same data may be encrypted by two keys, one of which may have low security. The possibilities of implementation errors are endless. And it typically boils down to careful design and consideration of possible outcomes.

3. **Trust model compromise**. Perpetrators at times attack the underlying trust model that forms the basis of the security plan. Trust model typically refers to the manner in which any software may deal with the platform or other services. More often than not software developers seem to trust the desktop on which the software may be running. This opens up a back door for malicious code and perpetrators to enter. Many a times the software may be developed with a certain set of assumptions, but the implementation may be on a platform that was designed with different trust assumptions in mind.

More specific details of cryptographic methods and security plans can be found in Menezes et al. (2010).

RSA Security Breach[4] ████████████████████████

In 1978, Ron Rivest, Adi Shamir, and Lenoard Adleman, three prominent mathematicians in the prestigious Massachusetts Institute of Technology, published a mathematical algorithm that is designed to digitally verify a sender's identity. This algorithm is dubbed "RSA", after the three men's last names. Subsequent to this historical event, Public Key Cryptography and the related Public Key Infrastructure have seen unprecedented growth in the world. Not to confuse Public Key Cryptography with its symmetric key cryptography, Public Key Cryptography uses asymmetric keys, or a public and private key pair, where each key of the pair can unlock or verify the other. Therefore, the keys cannot function alone, and must be used in pairs.

Soon following the disclosure of this algorithm, the three mathematicians founded the company RSA Data Security in 1982. Subsequently, RSA data security matured with the Public Key Infrastructure, and established well known subsidiaries such as the digital certificate authority Verisign, and e-commerce security vendor Xcert International. Through these establishments and acquisitions, RSA data security has built a lucrative portfolio of secure authentication and encryption products.

Among many of its products, RSA Data Security's most prominent products include the RSA BSAFE cryptography libraries and the SecureID second factor authentication token. The RSA BSAFE cryptography libraries contained numerous asymmetric cryptography algorithms, key management suites, and development kits, which can all be used to integrate the RSA cryptography into various applications.

Conversely, the RSA SecureID second factor authentication token is a hardware token based authentication system that allows an organization to authenticate a user by the value displayed on the token. While the hardware token may not sound like a product manufactured by a company

---

[4] Acknowledgements are due to Dan Han of Virginia Commonwealth University for his contribution to this section.

focusing on mathematics and encryption algorithms, the RSA SecureID token is the company's implementation of its cryptography algorithms. The SecureID system is composed of a server and a number of software or hardware tokens, or key fobs. These tokens are time synchronized with the server, where both the server and the token will generate a set of challenge-response access codes based on the AES-128 cryptographic algorithm on a timed interval. The challenge-response access codes are usually generated every 30 or 60 seconds. In order to authenticate to an RSA SecureID protected system, the user holding the token must enter the generated access code on the token at the specific time of authentication, as well as an assigned pin. The access code calculated by the server and the token are generated from a unique number called the seed record, the seed record is used in conjunction with the time of day and date, these values are then used in the RSA algorithm to calculate the access code for a particular token at any given point in time.

Coupled with these unique technologies are RSA Data Security's ingenious marketing campaigns. The company recognized that the association between the name RSA and asymmetric cryptography, and fully utilized the name to brand all of its products, from the smallest set of cryptographic algorithms all the way to its SecureID authentication systems. The company leveraged the brand recognition and was able to capture the business from various large enterprise customers. Further, to improve its reputation as a de facto power in the information security arena, the company sponsors and hosts the annual RSA conference in the San Francisco bay area, and is considered one of the premier events for cryptographers and information security professionals all around the world.

Equipped with a unique line of products and a good marketing campaign, the RSA Data Security's products are among some of the most popular with organizations worldwide, and RSA Data Security enjoyed a commanding lead in the asymmetric cryptography and online digital identity market, with its SecureID product occupying over 70% of the market in over 30,000 organizations worldwide.

In the late 1990s and early 2000s, with emergence of organizational information security and various national and international regulations that require two factor authentications, the multi-factor authentication and security market has rapidly grown into a lucrative market, with this advantage, RSA was able to increase its revenue by well over 50% in the early 2000s. Most of the revenue growth can be attributed to the company's SecureID tokens, as more organizations are realizing the importance of compliance and security. However, as time went on, new and improved technologies are developed and served as substitutes for the RSA's cash cow, the SecureID products. Many new technologies such as biometrics and smartcards are becoming increasingly affordable and easier to manage for organizations, which prompted some slow shift in the industry toward these more convenient and less expensive technologies. As a result, RSA realized that it must diversify in order to sustain its growth strategy.

In fall of 2006, several high profile and arguably failed acquisitions later, and after leading the online digital identity and security field for over two decades, the cash strapped RSA Data Security found itself in the crosshairs of multiple corporate predators. Among the hunters, one of the most prominent was EMC, the largest enterprise information and storage management company in the world. At the time, EMC CEO Joe Tucci believed that "Bringing RSA into the fold provides EMC with industry-leading identity and access management technologies and best-in-class encryption and key management software to help EMC deliver information lifecycle management securely." Despite the presence of multiple big name competitors such as Symantec and Cisco, EMC outbid the competitors and acquired RSA Data Security for a whopping $2.1 Billion, which valued the RSA stock at a shocking $28 per share, which is almost $10 per share over the market price. Soon after the acquisitions, RSA Data Security was rebranded as RSA Security, the security division of EMC. Under EMC's leadership, the new RSA focused on identity management, authentication, and professional security services. In the following years, RSA, acting on behalf of EMC subsequently acquired a couple of small companies that focused on file and data security, while attempted to diversify its security business beyond Internet identity management and second factor authentication.

The post-acquisition RSA operated as a subsidiary, or a separate company of EMC, where both companies had different presidents and hierarchies. Despite the fact that RSA has to report up to EMC, EMC allowed RSA much freedom to innovate and develop its products and offerings. In the subsequent years following the acquisition, RSA focused on areas such Incident and Event Management and Data Loss Prevention. Both technologies have assisted RSA to diversify its business, and have received generally positive reviews from the critics worldwide. As a result, growth was continuingly observed with RSA, as the company had 14 – 19% annual increases in annual revenue within the latter half of the 2000s. However, while these new ventures and products were able to help RSA diversify its portfolio, RSA still relied heavily on its SecureID product for revenue.

On March 17, 2011, RSA shocked the world by announcing that hackers were able to compromise an undisclosed set of information through an extremely sophisticated attack. Further, the company warned its users to take extra precautions in safeguarding their SecureID serial numbers, as the attack could reduce the effectiveness of the SecureID products. The company chairman Art Coviello stated that the attack was a form of Advanced Persistent Threat, which refers to highly sophisticated cyber espionage conducted by a group of hackers. Although no additional details were immediately announced, the security community speculated that the seed numbers used in the generation of the SecureID access codes were stolen, as RSA also keeps a database that contains these seed numbers, aside from the organizations that use SecureID. The announcement of this compromise has effectively put the hundreds of thousands of enterprises using SecureID to panic, as flabbergasted IT and security professionals in these organizations increased its monitoring and began to re-evaluate their implementations of the SecureID system.

With rumors and speculations flying around, organizations relying on SecureID authentication grew increasingly nervous as the time goes on, not sure how to properly deal with this situation, or even what is truly involved in the compromise. The answers many were seeking for was disclosed with a set of private security analysts on April 1, and subsequently to the public on April 4, 2011. According to an RSA spokeswoman, the breach was a result of a spear phishing attack.

A spear phishing attack is similar to phishing, which relies on social engineering techniques to trick the victims. Typically, phishing and spear phishing are conducted through emails or phones, where an attacker masquerades as someone else, and through a convincing message delivered to the victim, the attacker is then able to lure the victim into performing actions that may lead to further security compromise. However, despite the similarities, there are fundamental differences that separate phishing with spear phishing. While phishing focuses on the masses by distributing spam phishing emails to many people within an organization, spear phishing tries to target a small group of people with more convincing and targeted messages, thus yielding higher probability of compromise.

In the case of RSA, the hackers were able to gain publicly available information on its employees' names and roles from various social networking sites, such as FaceBook and LinkedIn. Subsequently, a targeted spear phishing email named "2011 Recruitment Plan" was sent to a small group of low level employees that contained an infected excel spreadsheet. However, all seemed to be safe as before the email reached its destination, the RSA spam filter was able to identify the email as spam, and automatically placed these emails in the trash folder of the intended recipients' inbox. Unfortunately, despite the early warning and quarantine of the malicious email by the company's spam filter, an employee retrieved the email from her trash folder and opened the attachment. The attached excel file contained a zero-day, or undisclosed vulnerability against the Adobe Flash software, which then proceeded to compromise her workstation and establish a backdoor for the attackers from within the RSA network. From this backdoor, the attackers installed a command and control toolkit named Poison Ivy RAT proxy on this employee's workstation, that enabled the attackers to remotely control the workstation, and further harvest authentication credentials from both the company's Active Directory user and application service accounts. Despite the lack of administrative rights, the attackers were able to leverage the vulnerabilities in the Adobe and Java applications to quickly escalate the privileges, and subsequently gained access to the highly credentialed IT administrators and process expert accounts. With these high level accounts compromised, the attackers were able to identify and access the internal database servers in RSA, identify the high value data, and subsequently copy these data to a staging server belonging to RSA. The staging server, being a non-production server, was not as heavily monitored, and provided the attackers a perfect hiding place to compress, encrypt, and ship the stolen data to the attacker's external server via FTP.

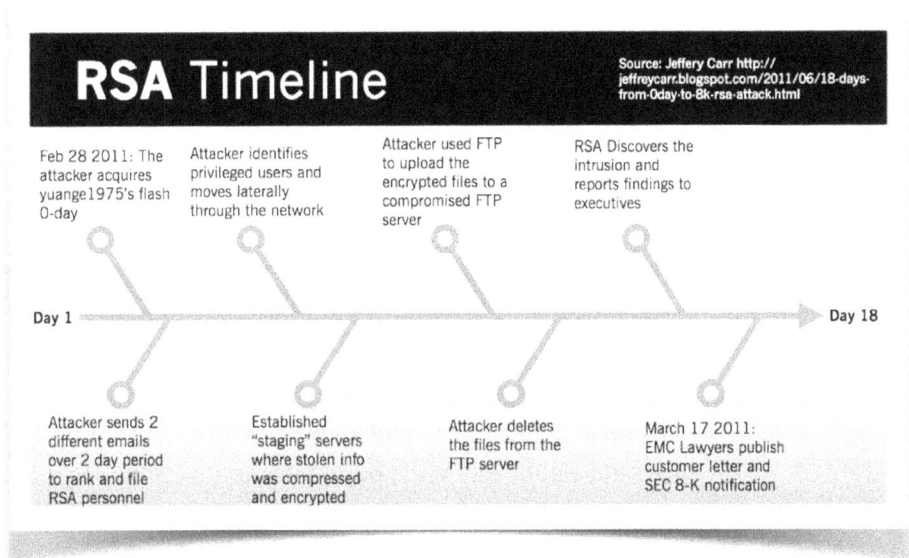

Figure 5.2, RSA breach timeline

Source: http://threatsim.com/2012/01/02/rsa-breach-timeline/

Fortunately for RSA, the breach was identified and contained relatively quickly thanks to its implementation of the NetWitness Security Information Event Management system, the system logs were correlated and the traffic was shut down within hours of discovery. However, despite the quick response, extremely sensitive data, including possible seed numbers for customer SecureID tokens are stolen. To further complicate the issue, the RSA engineer Uri Rivner has stated that the attackers may have compromised the RSA systems for months, but were waiting for the right opportunity to strike.

In hindsight, it is clear that although RSA deployed multiple technical controls, such as the email spam filter and least administrative rights, it was not well prepared against an attack against the informal realms of security, such as the human. Despite the fact that RSA was able to detect the breach when the data left the organization, this avoidable breach still cost RSA an enormous amount of data. Further, perhaps more importantly, the reputation and credibility for SecureID, RSA, and EMC have been significantly damaged, and with the SecureID seed values compromised, it is unclear how organizations around the world or SecureID's competitors will respond. Faced with scrutiny from both media and its customers, RSA suffered a detrimental blow from this incident. For a company that specializes in security, and heavily relies on its SecureID product line as its cash cow, the future of SecureID and RSA are up in the air.

Summary

In this chapter the basics of encryption have been presented. The historical perspective helps in systematically positioning the role of single key and public key encryption techniques. Differences between legitimate and fraudulent encryption methods are explored. Finally an analysis of cryptographic methods and development of a security plan for the organization is presented.

Six

6. Security Policies

The Basics

Cybersecurity is no longer simply a concern for only IT department staff. Today's business and IT environment demands that cybersecurity issues and practices be raised to the enterprise level with visibility and attention from business executives. This elevation in the visibility of cybersecurity is driven by many factors. Firstly, there is no question that information systems are ubiquitous in modern businesses. It would be difficult to find many significant business processes that do not rely on information systems to some degree. A good example of the influence of information systems on business practices is **Enterprise Resource Planning (ERP)** systems. In many cases, an information system is designed around the requirements of a business process. However, implementing an ERP frequently results in a business adapting their business processes to match the way they are designed in the system. Therefore, considering the importance of information systems in the successful operation of modern business, the integrity and availability components of cybersecurity become extremely important at an enterprise level. Additionally, cybersecurity importance and challenge has increased as IT has grown beyond the four walls of the enterprise, making reliance on strong perimeter security less effective. Information systems frequently interface with those at external business partners and customers. Many business activities are outsourced, putting company data and systems in the hands of external parties. A key driver for business executives focusing on cybersecurity is the growing landscape of compliance and regulatory requirements. Violating the requirements, such as those related to personal information, with poor security practices, can cause significant damage to a business through heavy penalties and reputational harm. Finally, the growing and evolving variety of security threats is an emerging concern with increasingly sophisticated hackers and malicious code. With all of these factors in mind, it is easy to see why cybersecurity topics need to be raised to the enterprise level and alignment must exist between business and security strategies.

Alignment

An important aspect of cybersecurity policy formulation is that of strategic alignment. There are four basic types of alignment that should occur between cybersecurity teams and the business (Kayworth & Whitten, 2010). These are:

1. Structural
2. Strategic
3. Relational
4. Cultural

Structural alignment refers to factors such as reporting relationships and matching a centralized or decentralized structure of the organization. For example, this may affect where you deploy your cybersecurity personnel. **Strategic alignment** basically refers to the degree with which priorities and activities are aligned. This includes a common understanding of differing perspectives and executive commitment to cybersecurity. **Relational alignment** refers to the existence of tight, productive work relationships between cybersecurity teams and various business stakeholders. Finally, **cultural alignment** refers to alignment of values.

Due to limited resources, information security team cannot protect everything, at least not to the same extent. It doesn't make sense to allocate the same level of resources to secure a database for tracking office supplies as should be devoted to a database containing sensitive employee payroll data. Therefore, a key component of aligning cybersecurity strategy to corporate strategy is to perform a **risk assessment** to determine the importance of company information systems and assets in terms of confidentiality, integrity, and availability. This risk assessment must be performed in collaboration with the business. Business executives have the responsibility for determining the level of risk tolerance of the enterprise, which will influence the outcomes of a cybersecurity risk assessment. Also, only the business managers can truly determine the needs of the information systems and data in their areas, so cybersecurity teams cannot live in a vacuum and make assumptions on where to focus their resources.

CIA and Cybersecurity Policy

It is critical to analyze information systems or assets with all three core security components in mind: confidentiality, integrity, and availability. For example, a company's public webpage is not considered confidential considering that all content is meant to be publically available. However, the availability of this webpage is critically important to the business for customer interaction. When many people think of cybersecurity, they frequently only focus on the confidentiality of information. If a risk assessment were performed with this narrow focus, the example of the company webpage might be overlooked, even though it has important security requirements for high availability. Alternatively, a small information system for an employee clinic at a corporate office is likely not going to be deemed business critical (i.e. low availability requirement). But, the system may contain extremely sensitive data considering HIPAA regulations (i.e. high confidentiality requirement). With these examples in mind, it is easy to see the importance of determining risk in terms of all security domains. These **risk assessment activities** will help promote alignment between security and the business by ensuring that cybersecurity teams are focusing their resources where the business needs them.

From another perspective, it can be argued that even though cybersecurity risk assessment is important, it is an operational activity and not a strategic activity (Dhillon, 1997). In the traditional risk-based approach, vulnerabilities or threats that are identified are addressed with mitigating controls to reduce risk and exposure. One potential issue resulting from this approach that can get in the way of strategic alignment is that business managers frequently see the mitigating controls as roadblocks that get in their way. This may even cause these business personnel to try to circumvent established controls, thus reducing the effectiveness of cybersecurity solutions (Dhillon, 1998). Additionally, applying mitigating controls to vulnerabilities discovered in a risk analysis frequently results in point solutions. A **business-aligned security strategy** is more of a top-down approach that begins by analyzing an organization's business strategies and goals instead of looking across an inventory of existing information systems and data. With this business focused, forward-looking approach, strategic business initiatives are executed with a security foundation. The result is a broad security strategy that addresses broader problems and future risk, as opposed to narrowly focusing on point solution to existing vulnerabilities. These practices will surely help promote security as a strategic enabler (Dhillon, 1997).

For more Information, please explore the following resources:

http://www.fbi.gov/about-us/cjis/cjis-security-policy-resource-center/view

http://www.sans.org/security-resources/policies/

Defining security policies

As previously mentioned, a business-driven security strategy can be thought of as a top-down approach to cybersecurity. Many cybersecurity teams take more of a bottom-up approach to security strategy that is more technology-centric. This frequently results in cybersecurity infrastructure that is overly complex and siloed. Also, an organization's security solutions will be more reactive rather than proactive if they are not looking ahead at future business strategies. The top-down approach will certainly help align information security strategy with business strategy since the security strategy will begin with the business. Rather than focus on security solutions for vulnerabilities in a specific technology, security organizations should begin by looking through the eyes of the business and view "security as a means to protect and enhance business processes" (see Baskerville & Dhillon, 2008).

Another issue that causes a disconnect between business executives and security teams is the significant difference in the way **investment criteria** are analyzed. Business investments are typically analyzed in terms of potential for revenue generation. This approach does not work for cybersecurity, considering the nature of investments in this area. Installing a new data loss prevention system, while important, is not going to generate revenue for the business. To address this challenge in communicating to business executives in terms of dollars, cybersecurity managers frequently try to quantify security investments in terms of risk avoidance. With the example of justifying funding for a new data loss prevention system, they will likely cite the average cost of a breach of customer personal information and how the investment will reduce the risk that this cost will occur. Cybersecurity investments are often pushed with scare tactics. Because of this challenge, business executives tend to undervalue security investments because they want to see a tangible return. Why would they choose to fund the new data loss prevention system when they can use that money to fund a new customer relationship management system that promises millions of dollars in increased sales?

What should go into a security policy?

A security policy should be no longer than is absolutely necessary. Some believe that policies are more impressive when they fill enormous binders, or contain hundreds or even thousands of policies. These types of policies overwhelm you with data, and are frequently advertised on the internet. But quantity does not equal quality, and it is the sheer amount of information in those policies that makes them useless. Brevity is of the utmost importance.

• A security policy should be written in "plain English." While, by nature, technical topics will be covered, it is important that the policy be clear and understood by the target audience for that particular policy. There is never room for "consultant-speak" in a security policy. If there is a doubt, the policy should be written so that more people can understand it rather than fewer. Clarity must be a priority in security policies, so that a policy isn't misunderstood during a crisis, or otherwise misapplied, which could lead to a critical vulnerability.

• A security policy must be consistent with applicable laws and regulations. In some countries there are laws that apply to a company's security practices, such as those covering the use of encryption. Some states have specific disclosure laws or regulations governing the protection of citizens' personal information, and some industries have regulations governing security policies. It is recommended that you research and become familiar with any regulations or standards that apply to your company's security controls.

• A security policy should be reasonable. The point of this process is to create a policy that you can actually use rather than one that makes your company secure on paper but is impossible to implement. Keep in mind that the more secure a policy is, the greater the burden it places on your users and IT staff to comply. Find a middle ground in the balance between security and usability that will work for you.

• A security policy must be enforceable. A policy should clearly state what actions are permitted and what actions are in violation of the policy. Further, the policy should spell out enforcement options when non-compliance or violations are discovered, and must be consistent with applicable laws.

Source: InstantSecurityPolicy.com

For more Information, please explore the following resources:

http://csrc.nist.gov

http://www.cert.org/encyc_article/

Figure 6.1, Security policy cycle

A proposed solution to bridge the financial communication gap between cybersecurity teams and business decision makers is to use **Monte-Carlo simulation** tools. Monte-Carlo simulations use a mathematical model to analyze financial decisions by simulating sources of uncertainty that affect their value. This model lends itself well to cybersecurity investment decisions since many of them are based on mitigating the risk of something that *might* happen. In other words, the actual return on investment of a cybersecurity investment is variable, based on the threats that it ends up preventing or mitigating. This is applied to cybersecurity by using several different risk criteria as input into the model, and the potential return on investment is plotted on a probability distribution graph. The mathematical model is quite complex. But, it is usually coded into software so the user does not need to be concerned with the mathematical technicalities. A key reason for using this approach to communicating information security investment criteria to the business is because financial decision makers are frequently familiar with using Monte-Carlo simulations to analyze financial decisions, so security teams will be "speaking their language".

Writing a security policy

There is no doubt then that a well-defined security strategy is necessary. Typically a security strategy gets reflected in a security policy. There are several ways in which a policy can be developed.

Donn Parker of SRI International has been a great influencer in the field of cyber security. In many ways he helped shape the field as it exists today.

For more Information, please explore the following resources:

See SANS security policy templates:

SANS Institute. (2013). Information Security Policy Templates. Retrieved from http://www.sans.org/security-resources/policies/

You might particularly look at Computer Security Division: Computer Security Resource Center linked to the following site:

National Institute of Standards and Technology. (2013). U.S. Department of Commerce. Retrieved from http://www.nist.gov/index.html

---

The case of Wikileaks[5]

The first question that comes to mind in the WikiLeaks/U.S. Military controversy is, what exactly is WikiLeaks? Clearly they have been making an impression, recently in the United States, but who are they? By their own definition, "WikiLeaks is a non-profit media organization dedicated to bringing important news and information to the public. We provide an innovative, secure and anonymous way for independent sources around the world to leak information to our journalists. We publish material of ethical, political and historical significance while keeping the identity of our sources anonymous, thus providing a universal way for the revealing of suppressed and censored injustices." In order to stay active the website relies on donations from supporters and information from "leaks" in military, government, and other prominent organizations and businesses. The steps that WikiLeaks goes through, or states they go through, on their website does appear to be in-depth and lends to the legitimacy of what they are publishing, in other words they are publishing real documents. But what the focus, in this particular situation, needs to be on is with the people who are leaking the information. More often than not the documents being leaked are considered classified, and should not be leaving company confines.

In 2010 WikiLeaks really came to the front page with several key leaks. Among other diplomatic releases made on WikiLeaks, in January of 2010, PFC Bradley Manning sent cables containing classified and secret information from a US embassy cable. He was eventually charged with transferring classified data onto his personal computer and communication national defense information to an unauthorized source. A total of 22 charges were added to the initial charges. Manning admitted to friend he had downloaded material from SIPRNet and then passed it onto WikiLeaks. It is estimated that over 250,000 United States diplomatic cables were included in the leak, approximately 15,000 of which have not been

[5] Acknowledgements are due to Elizabeth Kregiel for contributions to this security

leaked, but the intention is to post those to the website as well.

Now, this is a difficult policy to write because I am not one hundred percent sure of what the United States policy is concerning IT security. From what I understand the policy that is currently in place is one that once you are granted clearance to certain material, you have access, but are not monitored to what you access and what you download.

Douglas B. Wilson, the Pentagon's lead communicator said:

"I think the most significant lesson to come out of this is that technology -- and particularly technology at the intersection of national security -- has outpaced the policy and the law necessary to address the unintended consequences," Wilson said.

"Classified information is classified information, and releasing that information is illegal," he said. "But I think that we have a lot to do in government to understand that we need to be focusing much more on policy and much more on the laws that we need to think about to address what have been very unintended consequences of technological advance."

Below are policies for the Defense Department that allow for monitoring within each access level, monitoring of downloading information, and an ethical policy which would hopefully deter any wrong doing.

Summary

In this chapter we have developed an understanding of benefits of security policies and strategies. We have also considered the rationale behind certain security policies and appraised the elements that constitute a given policy. How security policies can be improved and properly aligned with business strategies is carefully considered.

Seven

7. Cyber Terrorism

The Basics

The convergence of terrorism and cyberspace is known as **cyber terrorism**. The term was first coined by Barry Collin in 1980. The aim of cyber terrorism is to disrupt critical national infrastructure or to intimidate a government or political establishments or civilian enterprise. The attack should cause violence, vandalism or enough harm to generate fear, for example explosions, plane crashes, or severe economic loss. The core characteristics of cyber terrorism include:

1. It is pursued to create destruction of nation's critical infrastructure

2. It can be executed by various means and involves computers and digital technology as main elements

3. It can affect government, citizens or other resources of high economic value

4. The act can be motivated by religious, social or political reasons

A large number of cyber terrorism acts conducted for social and political reasons have come to light in past few years. In 1996, a hacker associated to White Supremacist group temporarily disabled the Internet Service Provider and its record keeping system in Massachusetts. Though the provider attempted to stop the hacker from sending out hate messages, the hacker signed off with the threat, "You have yet to see true electronic terrorism. This is a promise." (Denning, 2000). Another example is of Kosovo conflict in 1999 when a group of hackers attacked NATO computer with e-mail bombs and denial of service attacks. The attack was a way to protest against NATO bombings.

Terrorists groups are increasingly using the Internet to spread their messages and to coordinate their actions and communicate their plans. There are hardly any networks that are fully prepared against all possibilities of threat. In comparison to traditional terrorism, cyber terrorism offers several advantages to terrorist groups. One, it is cheap, and can be executed from any part of the world. Two, the terrorist can be anonymous. Three, it doesn't put a terrorist life to risk. Four, the impact can be catastrophic, and five, white collar crime gets more attention. However, terrorists could face few hardships as well in executing cyber terrorism. First, the computer systems may be too complex for them to cause the desired level of damage. Second, some terrorists may be interested in causing actions that lead of loss of lives; cyber-attacks may usually not lead to loss of life. Third, terrorists may not be inclined to try new methods of sabotaging a system.

Some useful links:

http://www.nato.int/structur/library/bibref/cyberterrorism.pdf

http://www.fbi.gov/stats-services/publications/law-enforcement-bulletin/november-2011/cyber-terror

---

System vulnerabilities ███████████████████████

In order to determine the threat of cyber terrorism, two factors need to be considered. One, whether there are potential targets that are so vulnerable that an attack could lead to severe damage or violence. The second factor is, whether there are groups who have the intention and capability to exploit the vulnerabilities (Denning, 2000).

Regarding the potential vulnerabilities, critical infrastructure has always been the target of cyberterrorists. There are multitude ways that these vulnerable resources could be exploited. A report by President's Commission on Critical Infrastructure Protection in 1997 states that the vulnerability of infrastructure has been increasing and cost of attacks has been decreasing (President's Commission, 1997). Moreover, even if the technical controls are robust enough, the possibility of insiders misusing the capabilities is always high. As stated by Denning (2000) Russia's state-run gas monopoly, Gazprom, was attacked by terrorists with the help from an insider. The hackers infected the system by Trojan horses and gained the control of gas flows into pipelines. With the increasing use of social networking sites at work, the risk of being exploited by insiders increases. By nature of the information exchange that happens on social networking sites, hackers could use it to find sensitive information and launch attacks.

Regarding the people who may have intentions to exploit the vulnerabilities, the question boils down to possessing skills and knowledge to execute such vicious plans. While the information and tools to launch cyber attacks may be available, it needs a very highly motivated person to execute it. To some extent, strict regulations could demotivate the attackers. In the US the Computer Fraud and Abuse act of 1984 (section 1030) makes unauthorized access a federal crime with harsh penalties if convicted.

In a study conducted by Naval Postgraduate School in Monterey, California, in 1999, three types of cyberterrorists were identified: **simple and unstructured, advanced and structured** and **complex and coordinated**. The study examined that an organization would take 2 to 4 years to reach advanced level, and 6 to 10 years to reach complex level. However, the group may reach to complex level sooner if they seek help of other elements in their capacity (Nelson, Choi, Iacobucci, Mitchell, & Gagnon, 1999).

In simple and unstructured capability, hackers attack individual systems using tools created by someone else. The terrorist organization possesses little knowledge, skills and command and control. In advanced and structured capability, the terrorist group is capable of launching attacks against multiple systems and have the ability to create their own tools. The organization possesses basic knowledge, skills and command and control. In complex and coordinated attacks, the goal is usually mass destruction and the attackers have a capability to create sophisticated tools. The group possesses highly technical skills, knowledge and command and control capabilities.

Cyberdefense

Given the possibility of being exposed to ominous threat of cyberterrorism, the need for precautions against cyberterrorism becomes critical. Unlike the traditional defense mechanisms against natural calamities, **cyberdefense** is hard to implement for several reasons. One, cyber terrorism attacks do not occur as frequently as natural disasters. Two, given the nature of sophistication of technology involved, it is difficult to forecast the proactive measures that should be implemented to combat the disruptions. Despite the difficulties abound, law enforcement agencies need to be prepared at their end to overcome the aftermath of cyber attacks.

As stated by the FBI, responsible law enforcement agencies should remain vigilant for any such attacks launched against nation's critical infrastructure. The agencies should be adequately funded, equipped and trained. Besides law agencies, citizens should behave responsibly and report any suspicious behavior. There is also a need for imparting public education on how to react to such unforeseen situations.

Post September 11, 2011, the US revised its national security strategies in general and created new strategies for combating cyber terrorism in particular. Being a high-tech nation, the US faces a realistic threat to its critical infrastructure. Some of the laws that were formulated to minimize this threat are **Cyber Security Enhancement Act of 2002** (adopted on May 8, 2002) and **The National Strategy to Secure Cyberspace** (released on February 14, 2003) which led to the establishment of **National Cyber Security Division** (NCSD). The Cyber Security Enhancement Act is an amendment to Homeland Security Act and calls for toughening federal government actions against cyber terrorism. Under this act, federal agencies are allowed to eavesdrop personal communications and monitor behavior of suspects who illegally attempt to access federal government computer systems. NCSD is geared towards identification and removal of security holes in national infrastructure. NCSD along with other agencies also trace and prevent subliminal threats (Kim and Hyun, 2007).

For more Information, please explore the following resources:

For more information on cyberterrorism laws, visit the following publicly available sources:

Cybersecurity Enhancement Act of 2013. (Referred in Senate) H.R.756.RFS. http://thomas.loc.gov/cgi-bin/query/z?c113:H.R.756:/

Department of Homeland Security. (2013). National Strategy to Secure Cyberspace.

http://www.dhs.gov/national-strategy-secure-cyberspace

http://www.dhs.gov/xlibrary/assets/National_Cyberspace_Strategy.pdf

http://www.dhs.gov/national-strategy-secure-cyberspace

Ensuring the safety of systems and data

The Federal Bureau of Investigation considers Information warfare and cyber terrorism as two different types of threats: while cyber terrorism is a kind of information warfare, an act information warfare may or may not be cyber terrorism. There are several definitions or connotations.

One of the earliest and broader definitions of Information warfare is by Thomas Rona. According to Rona, "The strategic, operation, and tactical level competitions across the spectrum of peace, crisis, crisis escalation, conflict, war, war termination, and reconstitution/restoration, waged between competitors, adversaries or enemies using information means to achieve their objectives" (quoted by Libicki, 1995).

Another definition by Haeni (1997) puts Information Warfare as "Actions taken to achieve information superiority by affecting adversary information, information-based processes, information systems, and computer-based networks while defending one's own information, information-based processes, information systems, and computer-based networks."

As per Libicki (1995), there are seven different forms of information warfare:

1. **Command-and Control Warfare (C2W):** According to Department of Defense (DoD), C2W is the strategy employed by military to implement information warfare during war; it integrates physical destruction and the objective is to degrade or compromise enemy's command and control structure. The decapitation is done to serve the nation's strategic objectives.

2. **Intelligence-Based Warfare (IBW):** The real-time feeding of intelligence into operations to target the battle space is known as IBW. This has more to do with the high-tech technology that sends the real time signals in the battle space and enables the military to take informed actions

3. **Electronic Warfare (EW):** EW targets communication channels by degrading the physical medium to exchange information. The attack is more targeted to compromise the network traffic

4. **Psychological Warfare (PSYW):** PSYW is aimed against human mind. The war could be launched to disrupt national will, opposite commander, opposite troops, or even culture.

5. **Hacker Warfare (HW):** This warfare is aimed to exploit the security holes in the information system. Hacker warfare vary considerably and could be launched from almost anywhere in the world. The intent could be to shut down the entire system, steal sensitive data, inject viruses and so on.

6. **Economic information Warfare (EIW):** Information warfare and economic warfare when executed together leads to EIW. It can lead to either information blockade or information imperialism. Information Blockade assumes the wellbeing of nations determined by the flow of information. By disrupting the accessibility to information flow, the aim is to cripple the economies. In contrast, information imperialism has to do with the trade. Usually companies retain the highly technical information in-house and command high price for the products or service they specialize in. Acquiring and maintaining these positions could be considered a war in case the intention is to keep other nations behind.

7. **Cyberwarfare:** Libicki (1995) states that cyberwarfare is by far the most broadly defined area and includes many forms such as cyber terrorism, or information terrorism. In comparison to traditional terrorism, information terrorism would target individuals by attacking their data files and the effect of compromises could be catastrophic.

For more Information, please explore the following resources:

Haeni, R. E. (1997). Information warfare: An introduction. The George Washington University Cyberspace Policy Institute. Washington, D.C.: George Washington University. Retrieved from http://www.trinity.edu/rjensen/infowar.pdf

Libicki, M. (1995). Chapter 1. What is information warfare? National Defense University. Washington, D.C.: Information Warfare Site. Retrieved from http://www.iwar.org.uk/iwar/resources/ndu/infowar/a003ch01.html

---

The INSLAW affair

During the 1970's the Department of Justice of the United States of America pursued various avenues to standardize management information systems. The goal of this search was to assist law enforcement offices across the country in the recordkeeping and tracking of criminal cases. To this end, the Law Enforcement Assistance Administration (LEAA) funded the development of the Prosecutors Management Information System or PROMIS. The design of the software was initially undertaken on a nonprofit basis by INSLAW, a corporation funded almost entirely through Government grants and contracts. During the Carter administration LEAA was terminated. Subsequently INSLAW became a for-profit corporation commercially marketing PROMIS. The new corporation made several significant improvements to the original PROMIS software which later became known as Enhanced PROMIS.

In March 1982, the DOJ awarded INSLAW with a ten million dollar three year contract to supply and implement the original public domain version of PROMIS at 94 U.S attorney's offices. The contract quickly became embroiled in bitterness over the ownership of the privately funded Enhanced PROMIS software. The DOJ claimed they had unlimited rights to the software even after a contractual modification in 1983. All attempts by INSLAW to resolve the matter were met with hostility by the DOJ. Eventually the DOJ canceled part of the contract and withheld at least $1.6 million in payments to INSLAW. As a result the company was on the brink of insolvency and was threatened by dissolution. The DOJ claimed that the case was a contractual disagreement that had been blown out of proportion, while the owners of INSLAW persisted with there belief that there was a high level conspiracy by the DOJ to steal the PROMIS software.

The allegations made by the proprietors of INSLAW centered on their belief that the contractual disagreement was intentionally concocted by the DOJ to force the company into bankruptcy. The investigation discovered high level officials including Edwin Meese and Attorney General Lowell Jensen were involved with these decisions. The insolvency of INSLAW would have forced the sale of all its assets, including Enhanced PROMIS to a rival computer company called *Hadron Inc*. The owner of Hadron Inc. was a Dr E. Brown who had previously worked with Attorney General Meese in the cabinet of the Governor of California Ronald Reagan. The ultimate goal of the conspiracy was to position Hadron and other companies owned by Dr. Brown to utilize the $3 millions worth of automated data processing upgrade contracts planned by the DOJ.

Several worn affidavits were obtained by the owner of INSLAW attesting to the fact that the Enhanced PROMIS software was criminally acquired by Dr. Brain for modification of the program for use in covert intelligence. Two of the sources for these affidavits came from Ari Ben-Menashe a former Mossad officer and Micheal Riconosciuto who has links with covert intelligence agencies and allegedly programmed the Trojan Horse subroutine (Colin Brown, "Spies, Lies and Inslawgate", and "CIA Computer Consultant Alleges Massive Conspiracy", TC Technical Consultant, August-September 1192, pp.6, 10, 11, and 13). The software was modified to incorporate a Trojan Horse subroutine that could be used by U.S intelligence agencies to open a backdoor into the systems when required. Subsequently the software was distributed to several federal agencies, including the FBI, CIA and the DEA. Later the software was sold internationally to 88 different countries, according to Riconosciuto these countries included Iraq and Libya.

In 1986, INSLAW filed a law suit against the DOJ. A year later, the Bankruptcy Court ruled that the DOJ had stolen the Enhanced PROMIS software through "trickery, fraud and deceit" (INSLAW, Inc, vs United States, 83 B.R 89, Bankruptcy District Court 1988 at 158, Findings 399) and further attempted to cause the liquidation of INSLAW. In 1989, Senior U.S District Judge W. Bryant upheld the $8 million judgment, made by Bankruptcy Court, against the DOJ. He ruled that even the uncontested evidence virtually compelled the findings of the Bankruptcy Court "under any standard review". He added:

> The Government accuses the bankruptcy court of looking beyond the bankruptcy proceedings to find culpability by the Government. What is strikingly apparent from the testimony and depositions of key witnesses and may documents is that INSLAW performed its contract in a hostile

environment that extended from the higher echelons of the Justice Department to the officials who had the day-to-day responsibility for supervising its work.

However, these rulings were overturned on narrow jurisdictional grounds in the Court of Appeals in 1991. The Court did not disturb any of the 399 findings of fact about the DOJ's malfeasance against INSLAW. In 1992, the U.S Supreme Court of Appeals declined INSLAW a hearing on the decisions made by the U.S Court of Appeals.

On September 10, 1992, the Committee on the Judiciary of the House of Representatives concluded a three year investigation into allegations of a high level government conspiracy to pervert the course of justice. The findings of the committee corroborated the rulings of the two lower federal courts. It believed that the INSLAW software was stolen by the DOJ and that the plans to harm INSLAW had began no later than the first month of the three year contract. According to evidence uncovered by the committee these plans were masterminded by the highest-ranking officials of the Justice Department. Further evidence was found that corroborated the testimony of the former covert intelligence agents. The private sector associates of the leadership of the DOJ illegally sold PROMIS software domestically and internationally. The software was sold to intelligence agencies around the world for financial gain and to further the intelligence and foreign policy objectives of the United States. The committee concluded that the conduct of the DOJ "clearly raises the specter that the Departments actions taken against INSLAW in this matter represents an abuse of power of shameful proportions".

The committee also probed allegations by newspaper journalist that the suicide of an investigative reporter, Mr. D. Casolaro was connected to the INSLAW affair. The lifeless body of Mr. Casolaro was found in a hotel. He lay in a bathtub with each of his wrists slashed seven times. He had just completed a manuscript of the INSLAW affair and had told his family that he would be traveling to Martinsburg to obtain the final crucial piece of evidence for his book. Mr. Casolaro met his death in Martinsburg and the manuscript of his book had vanished. The case was judged as suicide. After much campaigning by Mr. Casolaro's brother the case was reopened, but the second verdict remained suicide. The committee believes that there is a link between Casolaro's death and the INSLAW affair.

Throughout the whole investigation the DOJ were either reluctant to pass information over to the Committee or blatantly ignored requests. Consequently, there were no charges brought against Mr. Meese, Dr. Brian or any of the other high ranking officials accused of conspiring to cause the bankruptcy of INSLAW. However, there is no dispute that the DOJ acted in bad faith and with hidden agendas.

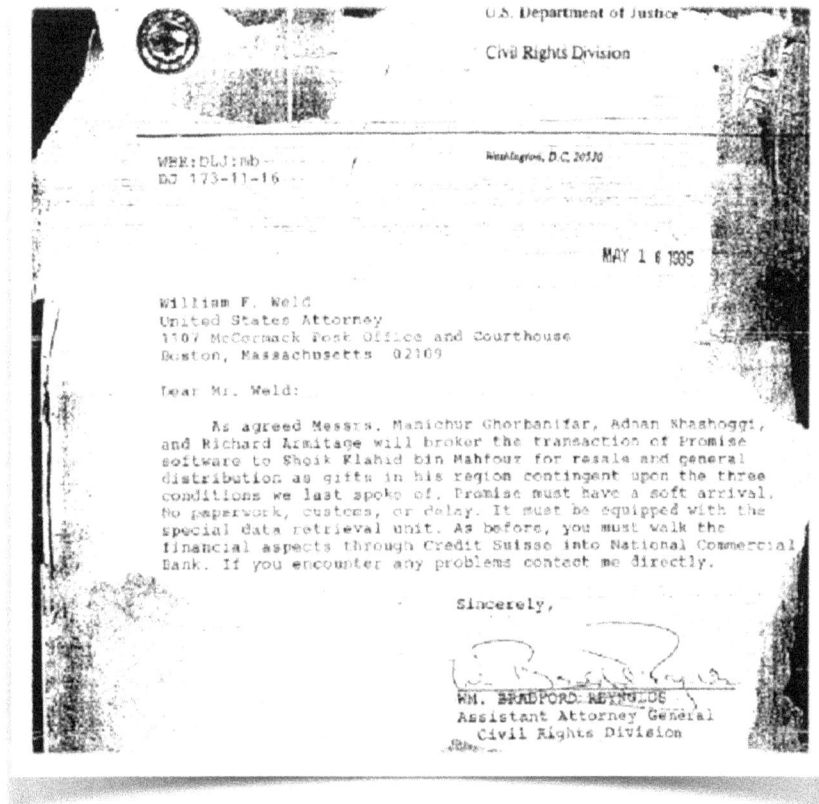

Figure 7.1, A letter related to the INLAW affair.

Source: http://gizadeathstar.com/2012/01/a-little-update-on-the-inslaw-matter/

Summary

In this chapter we have examined how cyber terrorism works. We have also evaluated the various methods adopted in information warfare. Various regulatory controls, their merits and demerits were also discussed. Cyber warfare is certainly emerging to be a serious threat and it is important to understand the motivation of perpetrators behind such acts. As a society this will allow us to be better prepared.

8. Cyber Detection and Forensics

The Basics

The term computer forensics originated in the late 1980s, when law enforcement used to refer it to the examination of standalone computer for the search of digital evidence of a criminal investigation. As the computer systems became more networked, computer forensics evolved to refer to the post-incident analysis of digital data. The National Institute of Standards and Technology (NIST) defines computer forensics as the application of scientific knowledge to identification, collection, examination, and analysis of digital data while maintaining the integrity of information[6]. Besides investigating suspect systems, collecting evidence, reconstructing events and analyzing current state of event, investigators use computer forensics for many other purposes, including:

1.   **Troubleshooting**: Forensics are applied to troubleshoot operational issues ranging from finding physical or virtual location of a

---

[6] See: http://homelandforensics.com/forensics.htm

host, recording current OS settings to resolving functional issues of an application.

2. **Monitoring**: Forensic tools are used for monitoring system and application logs for the identification of policy violations, auditing etc.

3. **Data Recovery**: Forensic tools and techniques can assist in accidental or intentional data deletion or data modification.

4. **Data Acquisition**: Forensic tools acquire data from hosts to be retired or redeployed.

5. **Regulatory Compliance**: Forensic tools help organizations to comply with regulatory requirements of protection sensitive information and maintain records for auditing purposes (Casey, 2000).

Computer Forensics Process

Computer forensics is a multidisciplinary field that cuts across several disciplines, including law, computing, information science, criminology and computer engineering. Regardless of the type of case under investigation, researchers categorize the computer forensic process into four phases:

1. *Evidence Collection*: The first step in forensic investigation is the collection and recovery of data related to the investigation of a crime. This data is evidence in the court of law. Investigators look for log files, caches, deleted files, router caches, switches, servers, Web 2.0 applications and other sources. Once investigators locate the data, they recover it by applying techniques to extract it in best possible state from where it is known to exist.

2. *Evidence Examination*: Once investigators recover the information, they need to preserve it for confirming the accuracy of the evidence collected. The NIST suggests that computer and network forensics answer two questions: does the collected evidence reflect all the pertinent information, and has someone changed the evidence since the time investigators collected it. Investigators can use several techniques, such as secure copying, storage mirroring and cryptographic digital signatures, to

ensure integrity, accuracy and authenticity of the data.

3.   *Evidence Analysis*: After investigators examine the data, they must analyze in in light of legal methods and techniques. The purpose is to analyze information that addresses the questions forming the basis of a forensic investigation.

4.   *Forensic Reporting*: Presenting forensic findings in court is the last and most difficult phase, because computer data have no physical existence. Moreover, most of the people in juries may have little to no knowledge about computers, networks, and digital information. Nevertheless, the forensic team needs to describe the actions taken, tools used, procedures followed and use simple graphics to present a digital case.

Creating an image for forensic purposes

Several tools are available that help in creating an image of the hard drive for forensic purposes. One such tool is CAINE (Computer Aided INvestigation Environment). If CAINE is being used then the following steps need to be followed (Note: all software's will perhaps require similar steps):

Booting CAINE. Insert the CAINE CD into the computer and boot the computer from the CD. In some cases BIOS settings may have to be changed.

Mount the external hard drive. Ensure that there is a connection between an external drive and the computer. This is the drive where the image will be saved. In CAINE version 2.0, a *Mounting Manager* option is available.

Create Image. In order to create an image the use of Automated Image and Restore (AIR) option needs to be used. This is built into the software. This option helps in creating an image of the hard drive.

Create a virtual machine. There are several available tools to create a virtual machine, including VMWare workstation. The software helps in creating a virtual machine, which can then help in running a live view of the hard disk.

Useful computer forensics links

http://www.caine-live.net

http://www.accessdata.com/products/digital-forensics/ftk

http://www.guidancesoftware.com/encase-forensic.htm

Case: Pharmaceutical counterfeit and Computer Forensics

An internal investigation started when a pharmaceutical company started receiving complaints from its representatives about the sales of normally high volume drugs fell down considerably. The investigation found that a large amount of the drugs was diverted in the United States through foreign countries and was sold through smaller distributors in the country. The initial analysis was analyzed and a forensic team was called.

The forensic team launched an investigation immediately and seized the diverted drugs form several locations. Besides the drugs, the digital devices including computers and other electronic devices were also seized.

New York Computer Forensic Services. (2006). Global Digital Forensics Case Study Drug Diversion.

Retrieved from http://www.newyorkcomputerforensics.com/learn/resources.php

Corporate Views versus Legal Views[7]

Law enforcement officials work with more restrictive rules than corporate employees. Corporate employees and law enforcement officials have different concerns regarding computer forensics (Solomon, 2005, p.9).

Corporate concerns primarily focus on detection and prevention. Increased news coverage of vulnerabilities in software and hardware has caused companies to prioritize security. Efforts are made to implement

---

[7] Parts are this chapter from here on are drawn from Bassett, R; Bass, L; O'Brien, P (2006). Computer Forensics: An Essential Ingredient for Cyber Security. Journal of Information Science and Technology Vol 3, No 1. Used with permission from the Journal of Information Science and Technology.

solutions for intrusion detection, web filtering, spam elimination and patch installation. Therefore, the corporate focus is on minimizing the potential damage caused from unauthorized access attempts through preventing, detecting, and identifying an unauthorized intrusion. This is accomplished by implementing security policies, as well as incident response and disaster recovery plans (Solomon, 2005, p.9).

In many corporate environments, incidents are not reported due to the issue of legal liability. There are some laws that hold management responsible for damages caused by a hacker, and a company may have to prove it took reasonable measures to defend itself from attack (Solomon, 2005, p.10). Management may fear the publicity received from an attack, as this could cause the company to lose customers. Furthermore, if incidents are reported the company risks having critical data and computers seized by law enforcement. An investigation could disrupt employee schedules and cause confusion, leading to interruptions in the work environment (Solomon, 2005, p.11).

Law enforcement agencies focus on investigation and prosecution. Each state has its own set of laws that direct how cases are prosecuted. Evidence has to be properly collected, processed and preserved in order for a case to be prosecuted. Law enforcement must deal with incredible amounts of data. Now that the Internet is involved, crimes can be committed from other states and countries, involving laws and jurisdictions of those regions (Solomon, 2005, p.11). Multiple jurisdictions and agencies can become involved in investigative and analytical activities, each of which may utilize its own procedures (*Forensic Procedures*, n.d.). This makes the law enforcement official's job that much more difficult.

General Methods in Computer Forensics

A Computer Forensic Specialist (CFS) must follow a rigid set of methods to ensure that computer evidence is correctly obtained. These steps are outlined in Table 1, which also introduces two critical terms: unallocated file space and file slack. The examination of unallocated file space is vital during a computer forensics investigation. When data is written to a storage device, data clusters from the File Allocation Table are allocated to store the data. But when the file is deleted by the user, the data is not erased. A 'delete' operation will incite these data clusters to become unallocated, but they will still hold onto the old data until the operating system reallocates these data clusters at a later time. The data residing in this unallocated file space can potentially contain fragments of files and subdirectories, as well as temporary files used by the application programs or operating systems. All of these types of data may contain sensitive information that can prove to be valuable during an investigation, and so it is necessary to uncover as much data from the unallocated file space as possible. Many criminals fail to recognize that the deletion process does not truly erase the sensitive data, and this is often where incriminating evidence will be discovered.

General Methods Used in Computer Forensics	
Method	Description
1 - Protect	Protect subject computer system from alteration, data corruption, virus infection, and physical damage
2 – Discover	Uncover all files: normal, hidden, deleted, encrypted, password-protected
3 – Recover	Recover as many of the deleted files as possible
4 - Reveal	Reveal the contents of hidden and temporary files
5 - Access	Access the protected and encrypted files, if legal
6 - Analyze	Analyze all relevant data, including data located in unallocated file space and file slack
7 - Report	Print out a listing of all relevant files, and provide an overall opinion on the system examination
8 - Testimony	Provide expert testimony or consultation, if required

File Slack is another source of vital data that criminals may overlook. When files are created, they are usually stored in clusters of fixed length. File sizes frequently do not match the cluster length exactly, and so the data storage space that exists from the end of the file to the end of the cluster is known as file slack. This file slack is often filled with randomly dumped data from the computer's memory, so there is the potential that it could include data related to network logon names, passwords, and private personal information. Since it is so important to access and reveal the contents of unallocated file space and file slack, software utilities used in computer forensics have been designed to efficiently and accurately uncover this important data.

Ethical Predicaments

These general methods show that sensitive data must be handled all the time in Computer Forensics. Consequently, there are many ethical dilemmas that a CFS must be prepared to deal with during an investigation. The most common ethical problem is managing the discovery of confidential data that is irrelevant to the case at hand. For example, if an investigator is searching through a mirror-image copy of a suspect's hard drive, he may come across a personal email that contains incriminating evidence of adultery or some other sort of inappropriate behavior that is not relevant to the ongoing case. The question of what to do with this information then arises. Computer Forensic Specialists must deal with this constantly, and the general code of ethics to follow is that this information must be ignored because it is not relevant to the investigation. However, it is not always easy to ignore this kind of information and any secrets that may be uncovered can weigh heavily on the mind of a CFS.

Acknowledgement of errors is another ethical dilemma that may be harder to overcome. If a CFS accidentally tampers with the data on the subject computer, this evidence would not be admissible in court, and the investigation would be compromised. Many Computer Forensic Specialists find it hard to admit these mistakes because one major screw up could lead to immediate unemployment (*Code of Ethics and Conduct*, 2004).

It is also necessary to remove all bias during an investigation. If a CFS goes into an investigation with the hope that the suspect is found innocent, he may ignore all evidence pointing towards culpability of the suspect and instead only report evidence that suggests innocence. This ethical problem can easily arise if the CFS has something to lose if the suspect is determined to be guilty.

Another ethical decision concerns the time-consuming nature of computer investigations. If the CFS has outside stresses to worry about, such as family problems, he may not spend the required time to thoroughly and completely investigate a subject computer. It is important to completely analyze the machine with proficient execution, and any insufficiencies in this endeavor can ruin the entire case in a split-second.

Maintaining control and responsibility for forensics equipment can also become an ethical issue. This can occur if the friend of a CFS suspects there is some fishy business going on with his computer and asks as a personal favor for the CFS to check out his machine and see what can be unearthed. This is unprofessional, unethical, and it shows a poor sense of responsibility for the forensic equipment with which Computer Forensic Specialists are entrusted. However, people are generally sympathetic towards their friends and will often act outside the bounds of logic and ethics to comply with a friend's requests.

Software Tools

Computer examiners use several different types of tools to identify and attain computer evidence. There are many different tools available to use for forensic analysis. The following is a description of three of the tools available.

One type of software available for forensic analysis is EnCase[8]. EnCase was originally developed for law enforcement personnel, but has matured to support commercial needs, as well. The EnCase Enterprise Edition is a network-enabled incident response system which offers immediate and complete forensic analysis of volatile and static data on compromised servers and workstations anywhere on the network, without disrupting operations. It consists of three components. The first of these components is the Examiner software. This software is installed on a secure system

[8] www.encase.com/products/ee_index.asp

where investigations and audits are performed. The second component is called SAFE, which stands for Secure Authentication of EnCase. SAFE is a server which is used to authenticate users, administer access rights, maintain logs of EnCase transactions, and provide for secure data transmission. The final component is Servlet, an efficient software component installed on network workstations and servers to establish connectivity between the Examiner, SAFE, and the networked workstations, servers, or devices being investigated.

These components work to provide the acquisition and analysis of volatile data on workstations and servers suspected to be compromised. This includes running applications, open files and other data in RAM, as well as acquiring and analyzing attached drive media, including files, operating systems artifacts, and data in file slack and unallocated spaces. It quickly isolates, identifies, assesses and rectifies both internal and external security breaches and provides non-intrusive forensic functionality to ensure that investigations withstand internal or external scrutiny regarding thoroughness, accuracy and authenticity.

In summary, the EnCase Enterprise Edition conducts comprehensive investigations, uncovering information and evidence pertaining to incidents that other tools cannot find. EnCase will find information despite efforts made to hide or delete it.

Also available is Paraben's P2 Examination Process[9]. This is a software suite consisting of nine different software applications, each of which takes a different role in the examination process. They are: Forensic Replicator, Forensic Sorter, E-mail Examiner, Network E-mail Examiner, Text Searcher, Case Agent Companion, Decryption Collection Enterprise, Chat Examiner, and PDA Seizure.

Forensic Replicator replicates exactly drives and media. Once that has been done, Forensic Sorter classifies data into different categories, recovering deleted files, and overall making the examination easier to manage, faster to process and easier to find the information desired. Next is the E-mail Examiner, which can recover active and deleted mail messages from America Online, USENET groups, Outlook Express, Juno, MSN mail,

[9] www.paraben-forensics.com/catalog/

and many others. Network E-mail Examiner will examine thoroughly network e-mail archives. Text Searcher is a fast and methodical searching tool which allows the examiner to search for specific terms in any text. It supports multiple languages, has full searching capabilities for specific file types as well as slack and unallocated space, and has an easy to use interface and report output. Case Agent Companion includes a file viewer which helps to organize examination results by case, logging all parts of analysis into a detailed log file.

Also included in Paraben's forensic software suite is Decryption Collection Enterprise, which recovers passwords and decrypts encrypted data. Chat Examiner analyzes chat logs. However, AOL Instant Messenger is not supported by Chat Examiner because it does not have traditional data stores or logs. The final piece of Paraben's suite is PDA Seizure, which acquires, views, and reports on data from a PDA.

Another software tool available is the Forensic Toolkit (www.accessdata.com/Product04_overview.htm). FTK offers law enforcement and corporate security the ability to perform complete, thorough computer forensics examinations, featuring powerful file filtering and search functions. Customizable filters allow the user to sort through thousands of files quickly to find the evidence needed. FTK is recognized as the leading forensic tool to perform e-mail analysis, recovering deleted and partially deleted e-mail. The Forensic Toolkit also will identify and flag known child pornography and other potential evidence files, as well as identifying standard operating system and program files. FTK also yields instant text search results, performs advance searches for JPEG images and Internet text, recovers deleted files and partitions, and targets key files quickly by the creation of custom file filters. It generates audit logs as well as case reports, and allows quick navigation through acquired images.

The EnCase Enterprise Edition, Paraben's P2 Examination Process, and Forensic Toolkit software packages have been highlighted because they illustrate the vast amount of functionality that is mandatory for investigating cyber crime. The methodologies of computer forensics are rigorous and thorough, and a software tool that can only create disk images is not sufficient for completion of the investigation. A dependable forensic software product should include high-quality implementations for every single method outlined in Table 1, as well as auditing capabilities so that the user can keep track of the details of the investigation. EnCase, Paraben's suite, and FTK are all examples of this brand of multifaceted forensic software that is necessary for viable use in the computer forensics process.

No matter what forensic software is used during an examination, it should be noted by its version and be used in accordance with the licensing agreement. Any software should be tested and validated for its forensic use by the examiner before an examination is undertaken.

Using EnCase to Capture a Criminal

The application of these software tools has helped bring many cyber criminals to justice. One recent case involved PayPal Inc., which is an online payment processing company. They observed that ten names were creating sets of at least forty accounts that were being used to buy expensive goods on eBay.com auctions. A mock PayPal site was discovered that was used by the criminals to grab user log-ins and passwords, and this led to the theft of tens of thousands of credit card numbers. The clever scam involved the criminals acting as sellers and buyers in the same eBay auctions, and then essentially paying themselves with stolen credit cards. A fraud investigator later discovered that the IP address of the people running the mock site exactly matched the IP addresses of the questionable PayPal accounts. When the perpetrators were eventually brought into custody, mirror-image copies of their hard drives were subjected to EnCase's keyword and pattern searching mechanism. Special care was taken to have EnCase uncover as much data from the file slack and unallocated file space as possible, and the fraud investigator John Kothanek reported that "We were able to establish a link between their machine's IP address, the credit cards they were using in our system and the Perl scripts they were using to open accounts on our system" (Radcliff, 2002). Alexey Ivanov and Vassili Gorchkov were the criminals accused of wire fraud, and Gorchkov was sentenced to three years in prison, while Ivanov was sentenced to four years in prison. The use of software tools such as EnCase alleviated some of the inherent complexity in gathering the necessary evidence to convict these two dangerous criminals.

Problems Computer Forensics Must Address

Most reliable forensic software tools are immensely helpful in stopping cyber crime. However, there are many problems that have not been solved in the field of computer forensics. Hard drive sizes are increasing exponentially. This has the twofold effect of not only dramatically increasing the duration of the disk-imaging process, but also of increasing the amount of time that must be devoted to data analysis, since more data is being uncovered. The real problem is that while the software may be great at uncovering the data, human ingenuity is required to mine through this huge pile of data and pick out the tidbits of incriminating evidence that may or may not even exist. This task is profoundly difficult to accomplish and the inevitable frustration a CFS faces here is not desirable. One possible solution to this obstacle is to find a way to automate much of the data analysis processing. However, coming up with a model or algorithmic procedure for this is a daunting task in itself, and this has yet to be resolved.

Another hindrance that a CFS faces is the limitations of the software tools in existence. These tools are quite reliable at disk-imaging and data discovery. However, the data recovery capabilities of the present tools are quite limited. The main problem is that "none of the software tools, commercial or non-commercial, are able to guarantee the recovery of unreferenced files" (Arthur, n.d.). These software tools are also plagued by limited extensibility beyond the standard desktop computer. Cyber criminals will jump on this vulnerability, and therefore the next step for this field is to implement reliable and high-quality forensic software tools for digital cameras, PDAs, routers, and so forth.

Commercial software tools are also a problem because software developers need to protect their code to prevent competitors from stealing their product. However, since most of the code is not made public, it is very difficult for the developers to verify error rates of the software, and so reliability of performance is still questionable. For example, one common way to calculate an error rate is to keep a history of all the bugs encountered and the severity of these bugs. However, if the source code is not open to the public, the developer could simply fix a bug without ever publicly documenting it, and so this bug would not be accounted for in the error rate (Carrier, n.d.). Therefore, the commercial interests of the software developers will often take precedence over the quality of software, and this is not good news for the CFS whose investigations are dependent upon the reliability of the software. The general mindset is that open-source forensic software would be an ideal fix for this conflict. However, most software developers are out to make a profit, and consequently they do not see many benefits in joining the open-source code movement.

This financial motivation is also strongly entwined with the major problem that corporations have with the field of computer forensics. The specialized tools used by a CFS are viewed as intolerably expensive by many corporations, and as a result many corporations simply choose not to invest any meaningful money into computer forensics. This trend amplifies cyber crime rates because "This leaves these companies and agencies unprepared to deal with and respond to computer-related security incidents that occur on their systems" (Isner, 2003). Education and training are the keys to solving this problem. Many corporations depend on the Internet for daily transactions, and they need to become more aware of the fact that security may seem like an expense, but in the long-run it will yield a profit by decreasing the amount of damage done by cyber criminals.

In addition to all these problems, Computer Forensic Specialists also must find a way to overcome the general lack of knowledge that may exist in a courtroom setting. Nothing is more frustrating than for a CFS to put in a painstaking number of hours scrutinizing every detail of a hard drive, only to find out that his efforts were fruitless because he could not convey his findings to judges and lawyers in an adequate manner. Part of this problem hinges on the general lack of awareness that still exists in the courtroom setting in regards to computer evidence. Many people still lack familiarity with common computer concepts, and so it is difficult to fully explain the depths of the investigative findings without getting overly technical. So in addition to mastering the software and hardware knowledge necessary to be a skilled CFS, it is also necessary to know how to clearly articulate important findings in the courtroom.

Conclusion

Computer forensics is an increasingly important field that requires one to possess an intricate mix of technical skills, legal knowledge, and ethical behavior patterns. Specialists in this field have very powerful software tools at their disposal which will uncover a myriad of data to be sorted through, and it is up to the specialist to figure out what the important facts are and how to present them appropriately in a court of law. Even though the software tools are generally praised for their effectiveness, the statistics show that an improvement in the overall methodologies used in computer forensics is required. The FBI has made it known that "in the year 2000 there were 2,032 cases opened involving cyber crime. Of those cases, only 921 were closed. Of those closed cases only 54 convictions were handed down in court" (Isner, 2003). This is an alarming statistic, but it should not be surprising considering that the field is still in its infancy. As technologies expand, more powerful and versatile software tools will be required, and more well-trained Computer Forensic Specialists will be needed because cyber crime is exploding and computer forensics is the vital discipline that has the power to control this outburst.

Nine

9. Ethics and Technology*

The Basics

Enormous and dramatically swift changes in Information Technology (IT) and Information Systems (IS) have created a global economy on an unprecedented scale, one that is perhaps much more pervasive than many had previously anticipated. The speed of this change has caught many companies as well as IT professionals by surprise. Many companies have had to undergo rapid restructuring to face new challenges and to take advantage of new opportunities, while IT professionals have had to concern themselves with a wide variety of hitherto unfamiliar concerns and issues, including those involving culture, ethics, intellectual property, and computer crime.

The last two decades have seen enormous and dramatic changes in the way we view and use information. These changes have had far reaching

* A version of this chapter was published in the proceedings of the 2001 BITWorld conference. Relevant sections have reproduced with permission of the Information Institute (www.information-institute.org)

effects, including, but certainly not limited to, the creation of a complex and vibrant global economy, and a sea change in the way we live, work and play. For corporations, profitability and survival are increasingly contingent upon an ability to successfully operate in this global arena. Technology has played a pivotal role in the creation of this global economy and will be a crucial determinant of success for organizations that operate within it. Although political boundaries between countries still exist, on a map that shows the real flows of financial and industrial activity, those boundaries have largely disappeared (Ohmae, 1989). Ties between nations and regions are tied more to business and economic expediencies rather than any alignment of political ideology. The transnational corporation has become commonplace, as companies use IS and IT to connect and manage enterprises that were often scattered all over the globe. The virtual corporation - a corporation that possesses no assets in the traditional sense - is increasingly making its presence felt as companies transport goods and services from all over the world to their customers, who are also all over the world. An increasing level of worldwide economic activity today depends on the operations of these organizations such as these (Egelhoff, 1991). Corporations in the United States and abroad now find themselves in a situation where the ability to compete efficiently and effectively in the global economy is critical to their short-term profitability and possibly their long-term survival. Thus the issues involved in global operations have both an operational as well as a strategic impact.

To a great extent, technology is responsible for the growth of the global market as well as the speed of this growth. It is also the single most essential tool that a firm can use to facilitate and manage global operations. Thus, without effective and efficient IT systems in place, companies would likely find it impossible to manage global operations profitably. As a result, in many instances, the cause is also the cure. We are all aware that technology can be used to bring about organizational change, to enhance a company's competitive advantage, and to bring efficiency to operations. For a company that operates in the global economy, technology can provide the additional benefits of overcoming barriers such as time zone differences, geographic separation, and training difficulties. Thus, changes and advances in information technology, including computers, telecommunications, and office automation have brought global markets and global competition to the doorstep of even the smallest companies (Cash et al, 1992, Neumann, 1992). No major industry has escaped the effects of this globalization. We buy clothes, automobiles, and lumber from overseas markets. Our grocery stores provide us with food from distant places. We bank at institutions that have a worldwide presence. Our homes are filled with products that have been manufactured in dozens of different countries. Nothing is really local anymore, and to many businesses, any place is just the same as any other place. As Jim Hoagland, an American newspaper columnist wrote, "anywhere is rapidly becoming everywhere."

To survive in today's complex and volatile marketplace, businesses must become information based (Drucker, 1988). The use of IS and IT to enhance a firm's competitive advantage, to change and streamline its organization structure, to bring efficiency to its operations, to cope with increased levels of complexity and uncertainty, has been researched and recognized (Cash et al, 1992, Neumann, 1992, Porter and Millar, 1979, Roche, 1992). IT and IS are the weapons of choice in this new battle for survival, and the caliber of a firm's IS will play a major contributing role in determining its continuing overall success. In the global marketplace, where the transnational, multinational, or virtual corporation operates, an additional requirement becomes evident: the ability to compete effectively in a global economy will depend not only on the effectiveness of the firm's IS, but also upon the global orientation of this IS (Ives and Jarvenpaa, 1991, Karimi & Konsynski, 1991). Since these organizations operate across products, markets, nations and cultures, they face problems and situations that are often far more diverse and complex than those faced by even the largest domestic firms (Egelhoff, 1991), and ethics certainly becomes a major issue. Nevertheless, to these organizations, the potential benefits of an effective global IS are enormous, as IT can provide tremendous advantages in overcoming barriers such as time zone differences, geographic separation and training difficulties. There is little doubt, therefore, that the issues relating to the management of global IS and IT, including those pertaining to ethical situations have become increasingly important to most organizations that have a global presence. As technology shrinks the world, fewer and fewer businesses will be able to escape the touch of the global economy in some form or other, and even smaller companies are likely to find that a global IS is essential for growth and survival (Neumann, 1992).

It is obvious, therefore, that the effective and efficient use of technology can and often does bring significant advantages to a company seeking success in global markets. However, the planning, implementation, and maintenance of these systems can be fraught with difficulties. The company and its IS personnel will in all likelihood have to overcome many hurdles if they are to be successful. Differences in cultures, languages, currencies, customs, values, legal and educational environments, are but some of the many areas where large variations can create new problems and concerns. IS personnel, like others in their company are thus faced with the doubly difficult task of 'thinking globally and acting locally.'

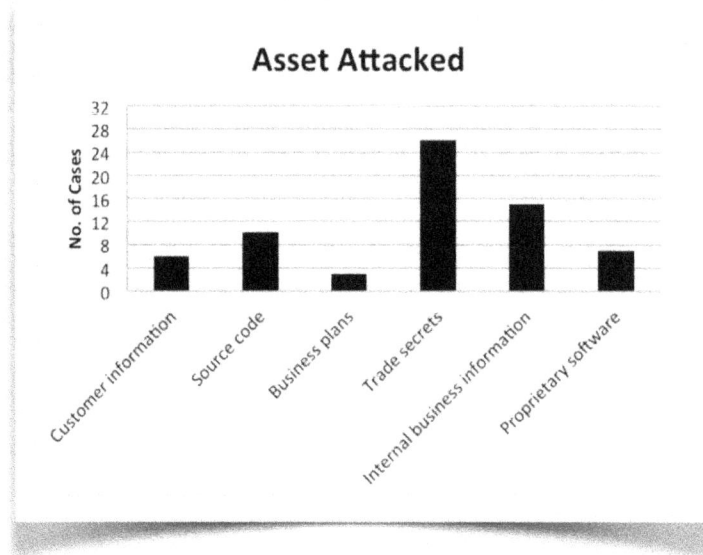

Figure 9.1, Type of asset attacked

Source: http://www.cert.org/

One area that can cause significant difficulties for IS personnel is the area of ethics. Another potential minefield is in the area of intellectual property. As the use of technology in the global arena increases rapidly, so does the potential for ethically nebulous situations. The intention of this paper is to examine the global framework in the areas of computer crime, intellectual property, and information systems ethics. The resulting analysis should provide IS personnel with some perspectives on what they might expect in the global markets. Figure 9.1 illustrates the types of assets attached based on a study by CERT.

Concepts regarding computer crime, intellectual property, and ethical use of technology appear to vary widely across the world. In a culturally diverse world that has increasingly become smaller through the use of technology, the potential for conflicts revolving around these three areas has increased dramatically. IS professionals will need a thorough understanding of a region's value system and cultural mores in order to operate effectively. This knowledge base will need to be acquired through education and experience.

Intellectual Property and Crime

The area of Information Systems (IS) ethics has been getting a lot of attention recently, And with good reason. Although many of the articles in the field address ethical issues pertaining to the use of IS and IT in the United States, they cover a lot of very valuable territory and provide useful insights that can provide direction in the examination of the issues from a global perspective. In the United States, both practitioners and educators in the field are agreed on the necessity for ground rules that govern the ethical use of Information Technology (IT). There is also a growing realization that we need to incorporate ethics into IS curricula (Cohen and Cornwell, 1994, Cohen and Cornwell, 1989, Couger, 1989).

The reason for all this concern is obvious. The unethical use of IS and IT is pervasive. It also seems to be growing at least as rapidly as the technology. In the United States, most states have laws against software piracy and unauthorized system access. Similar laws exist in other countries as well. Nevertheless, many users pay little or no attention to these laws. The Software Publishers Association (SPA) estimates that in 1997, global revenue losses due to piracy in the business application software market approached $11.4 billion worldwide (Gopal and Sanders, 2000). Studies such as those by Moore and Dhillon (2000), who examined the extent of software piracy in Hong Kong, serve to lend credence to the belief that the violation of intellectual property law occurs all over the world on an unprecedented scale. This remains true even though legislation providing penalties for such violations may be on the books. After all, there are many reasons that prompt the violator to copy software. For instance, while it may cost many millions of dollars to develop the initial copy of the software, it costs virtually nothing to produce a pirated copy. The high costs of legitimate copies, and the fact that constant updating of software (at considerable expense) is necessary in order to remain current, may well be another motivator for software piracy. This is especially true for countries where the per capita income is low, and where the cost of a legitimate piece of software is prohibitive in local currency terms. The enormous price differential between legitimate and pirated versions of software can often be the primary reason behind the piracy.

The problem of piracy and unethical use of IT can be found closer to home as well. Studies of ethical practices in business and in schools indicate distressing behavior patterns (Bloombecker, 1991, Machan, 1991, Stark, 1993). An examination of software copying policies at universities in the United States discovered attitudes toward software piracy that can generously be described as woefully lax, *especially among faculty* (Athey, 1990). Other studies tend to confirm this rather conclusively (Cohen and Cornwell, 1989, Im and van Epps, 1991, Reid et al, 1992, Wickham et al, 1992). Another study showed that many IT users believed that unethical use of IT could actually help them succeed in their business endeavors successful (Davis and Vitell, 1992). There seems little doubt that ethical standards in IS may well be on the decline. Yet another study showed that students possessed fewer and lower ethical standards than IS professionals in managerial positions (Wood, 1991). Sooner or later, of course these very same students will enter the workforce, complete with their severely crippled ethical standards.

Let us also not forget that unethical use of IT does not consist solely of software piracy or the violation of intellectual property laws. The umbrella of ethical use covers a much larger area. In reality, perceptions of what is ethical and what is not vary widely not just within the United States, but all over the world. The fact of the matter is that people tend to rely heavily on their personal values when deciding what is ethical or unethical behavior (Kreie and Cronan, 2000). It seems logical to conclude that the variation can only increase as we move into the global market with its wide variety of cultures and social values, which of course heavily influence personal values and mores. Another very disturbing fact that emerges from studies is that even among people who do not have difficulty in grasping what constitutes unethical use of IT and what does not, there is a tendency to ignore these distinctions (Athey, 1990, Wickham et al, 1992). That is, they know it's wrong, but they do it anyway.

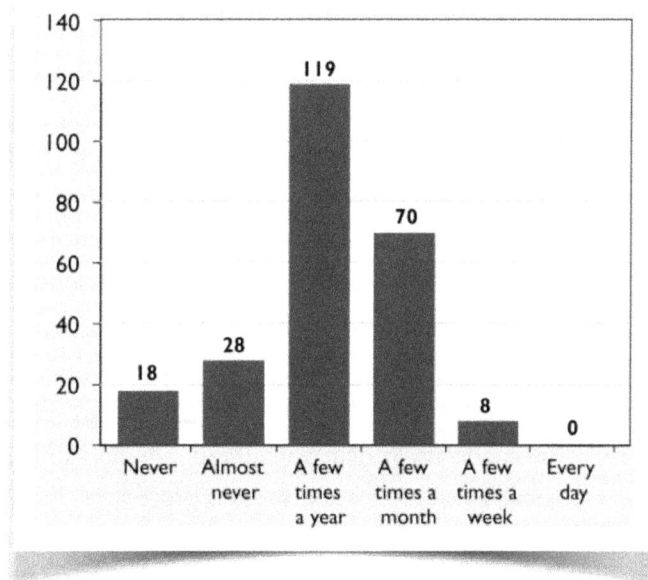

Figure 9.2, Frequency of buying pirated software in Hong Kong (Source Moores and Dhillon, 2000)

In an extensive study of software piracy in Hong Kong, Moores and Dhillon (2000) report (also see figure 9.2):

There is strong agreement from the respondents in terms of buying pirated software in the context of high availability of pirated software, low censure for buying, and the high cost of legal software. Reversing the contexts (i.e., low availability, high censure, low cost) resulted in a significant shift in their responses, suggesting the potential to reduce software piracy by addressing these three issues. However, only the cost issue showed the expected switch from agreement to disagreement, suggesting that a campaign aimed at this issue alone is likely to be more successful than reducing availability and increasing punishment for buying pirated software. Pg 92.

No one single factor can be held responsible for the current and projected crisis in Information Systems Ethics. For instance, the massive proliferation of inexpensive computing power has actually created an environment without which some crimes and unethical acts would never have been possible (Neumann, 1991). The software piracy epidemic has only been possible because of the huge growth in the number of microcomputers in use (Solomon and O'Brien, 1990). Because this tremendous growth in computing power has been coupled with a similar decline in costs, many more people today have ready access to enormous quantities of information and the inexpensive means to manipulate it.

In addition, new IT often creates situations with ethical implications that have no precedent. This causes obvious difficulties for IT users. Many IT users, both individual and organizational, do not possess the mechanisms to deal with these new and unfamiliar situations. Previously established codes, policies and procedures may often be so dated as to have no relevance to today's IS ethics issues. The management of IT can also be fraught with ethical dilemmas (Parker et al, 1990). Information created and stored electronically is easier to access, manipulate, or destroy without authority or permission than information that is stored on hard copy. Concerns of privacy, security, and theft of information have become increasingly relevant concerns for today's IS manager.

The use of computers and sophisticated communications equipment has changed interpersonal communication. Because so many human interactions no longer involve personal, face-to-face contact, decisions are often made with less thought and consideration. The potential for unethical conduct increases simply because not enough time is devoted to careful consideration of all the ramifications of a particular act. All too often, information sharing conflicts with concerns of confidentiality and privacy, and the lack of access security can often make unethical use far too easy.

Even IS professionals sometimes find it difficult to agree on what is ethical use of IT and what is not. In fact, many of the legal and ethical issues regarding the use of IT still remain cloudy. Although most states now have laws to deal with the possible criminal use of IT, almost every new case brings to light ethical and legal aspects that have not previously been encountered or examined. Many of these situations find IS professionals confused about the issues and at odds with others in their profession (Denning et al, 1992).

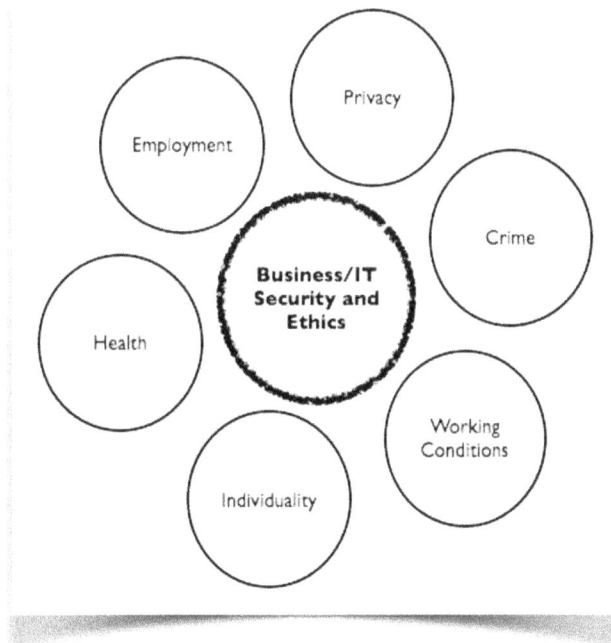

Figure 9.3, Interplay between security and ethics

ACM Code of Ethics and Professional Practice

Software engineers shall commit themselves to making the analysis, specification, design, development, testing and maintenance of software a beneficial and respected profession. In accordance with their commitment to the health, safety and welfare of the public, software engineers shall adhere to the following Eight Principles:

1. PUBLIC - Software engineers shall act consistently with the public interest.

2. CLIENT AND EMPLOYER - Software engineers shall act in a manner that is in the best interests of their client and employer consistent with the public interest.

3. PRODUCT - Software engineers shall ensure that their products and related modifications meet the highest professional standards possible.

4. JUDGMENT - Software engineers shall maintain integrity and independence in their professional judgment.

5. MANAGEMENT - Software engineering managers and leaders shall subscribe to and promote an ethical approach to the management of software development and maintenance.

6. PROFESSION - Software engineers shall advance the integrity and reputation of the profession consistent with the public interest.

7. COLLEAGUES - Software engineers shall be fair to and supportive of their colleagues.

8. SELF - Software engineers shall participate in lifelong learning regarding the practice of their profession and shall promote an ethical approach to the practice of the profession.

Source: http://www.acm.org/about/se-code#short

Many professional IS organizations today have codes of ethical conduct and behavior. They include the Association for Computing Machinery (ACM), the Association of Information Technology Professionals (AITP), and the Association of Computing Professionals (ACP). Some of these codes have been in existence for well over 30 years. Nevertheless, there is no widely accepted set of codes and guidelines that would apply in even a domestic setting, let alone a global one. Technology has grown in complexity and use to such an extent that even the more recently developed codes of conduct can't possibly address the bewildering range of possible situations involving ethical conflict. Then too, because computer use today is so pervasive, the majority of people who should be targeted by these codes of conduct do not belong to the professional organizations that developed them. In fact, many IS professionals do not belong to any professional organizations. Obviously, a large proportion of IT users are never exposed to any code of conduct.

The magnitude of the concern that exists today regarding IS ethics is directly related to the rapidly growing number of IT users. For instance, software piracy didn't seem to be much of a problem until microcomputers made their first appearance about 10 years ago (Solomon and O'Brien, 1990). The proliferation of microcomputer use is most definitely not limited to IS professionals and students (Wood, 1993). As early as 1984, in his testimony before the US Congress, computer security expert Robert Campbell accused the computer industry of failing to develop the necessary ethical framework for IT use. He went on to say that the technology had already breached the boundaries of the professional arena and proliferated into the public domain. He was right. The use of microcomputers today has permeated into almost every human activity, and the number of people who use IT on a day to day basis, at home and at work, is growing explosively.

Implications and Conclusions

Let us now briefly summarize our position. We live in a global economy, one that has largely been created and nurtured by the rapid growth in Information Technology. This technology, then, is the common thread that ties together a world that is disparate in many other ways – culturally, economically, and linguistically, just to name a few. But concerns of privacy, security, theft of information, malicious destruction, and intellectual property rights have become increasingly relevant today, and as a result this common thread shows imperfections and weaknesses, as it is misused, ill used, and even abused. Why does this happen and what, if anything, can be done about it?

Not all the reasons for the misuse of IT (we use this term to cover a wide variety of maladies, including crime, piracy, intellectual property violations, unethical use, etc.) can be laid to rest at the doorstep of globalization. As studies have shown, even relative homogenous populations with high per capita incomes have problems of IT misuse. Globalization and a multicultural economy certainly make the issues more complicated, however.

The misuse of IT occurs for all the reasons outlined in the previous section. But cultural differences can make a lot of difference as well. For instance, the concept of equating 'lawful' and 'just' is usually more prevalent in western society. This, of course, has enormous implications for those interested in the enforcement of copyright and patent legislation. Even this legislation varies from one part of the world to another. A study by McConnell International (2000) found that only nine of 52 nations surveyed have amended their laws to cover more than half of the cyber crimes that need to be addressed. Their conclusion was that the law only provided a small part of the answer; corporations would need to provide themselves with self-protection as a first line of defense. They also concluded that a global patchwork of laws would leave large gaps since crimes would not always be defined in a similar manner across all jurisdictions. The study suggested three steps that can be taken to counter cyber crime. (1) Companies should secure their own information, (2) Governments should assure that their laws apply to cyber crimes, and (3) Firms, governments, and civil society should work cooperatively to strengthen legal frameworks for cyber security.

Other studies also provide insights into the reasons behind IT misuse. In their study, Gopal and Sanders (2000) showed, among other things, that the price of the software is inversely related to the degree of piracy and also that the incentive for governments to enact and enforce copyright laws is related to the size of the domestic software industry. They concluded that a policy that focuses purely on enforcing intellectual property rights would have limited success at best. The war against software piracy cannot be won without addressing the current draconian pricing policies of many of the major software companies. The authors suggest a 'global price discrimination' policy as a tool against software piracy instead.

Obviously, this is an area that is enormously complex. The interplay of global economic forces, moral and cultural differences between regions, nations, and individuals, personal values, the law, justice, economic discrimination, and a host of other issues makes this an area that is at once immensely convoluted as well as enormously interesting. Although because of space constraints this paper must end here, the discussion can obviously go on forever!

10. Case. HIPAA - help or hindrance[*]

The Basics

In today's health care environment, whether it may be patient, provider, broker or third party payer, personal health information can be accessed from multiple locations at any time from any of these integrated stakeholders.   The spirit of HIPAA is to promote a better healthcare delivery system by broad and sweeping legislative measures. One way this can be accomplished is by the adoption of lower cost Internet and information technology.   It is clear the Internet will probably be the platform of choice in the near future for processing health transactions and communicating information and data. Therefore, information security is of paramount importance to the future of any health care program.

Whether you are a large healthcare provider/insurance company or a small rural physician practice, benefits consulting firm, or TPA, you will

[*] This chapter is a contribution by Jon Vosburg.

have to consider a security strategy for personal history information (PHI) to be in compliance with HIPAA. Otherwise, your operation could be subjected to hefty fines and potential lawsuits.

Requirements

In 1996, the Health Insurance Portability and Accountability Act (HIPAA PL 104-191) was passed with provisions subtitled Administrative Simplification. The primary purpose of this Act was to improve Medicare under title XVIII and XIX of the Social Security Act as well as the efficiency and effectiveness of the healthcare system through the development of a health information system with established standards and requirements for the electronic transmission of health information. HIPAA is the first national regulation on medical privacy and is the most far-reaching federal legislation involving health information management affecting the use, release and transmission of private medical data (Bogen, 2001).

As previously mentioned, HIPAA has important implications for all healthcare providers, payers, patients, and other stakeholders. Although the Administrative Simplification standards are lengthy and complex, the focus of this section of the paper will examine the following areas regarding PHI privacy and security:

- Standardization of electronic patient administrative and financial data

- Unique identifiers for providers, health plans, and employers

- Changers to most healthcare transaction and administrative information systems

- Privacy regulation and the confidentiality of patient information.

- Technical practices and procedures to insure data integrity, security, and availability of Healthcare information.

HIPAA mandates a set of rules to be implemented by health providers, payers, and government benefit authorities as well as pharmacy benefit managers, claims processors, or other transaction clearinghouses. It is important to note that HIPAA security and privacy requirements may be separate standards but they are closely linked. *Privacy* concerns what information is covered, and *security* is the mechanism to protect it. The Privacy and the proposed security standards of

HIPAA can apply to any individual health information whether it is oral or recorded in any form or medium. The information identifies the individual or can be used to identify the individual.

This is a significant departure from the previous draft rules that covered only electronic information. As a much broader definition of the law, it will require a significant change in the way health information is handled, disseminated, communicated, and accessed (Bogen, 2001).

Compliance and Recommended Protection

The first place to begin is to examine PHI vulnerabilities and exposure by completing a business impact analysis and a risk assessment to determine compliance with HIPAA. This should include a:

- Baseline Assesment: The baseline assessment inventories an organization's current Security environment with respect to policies, processes and technology. This should include a thorough assessment of information systems that store, transact or process patient data.

- Gap Analysis: The goal of the Gap Analysis is to compare the current environment with the proposed regulatory one in terms of level of readiness and the determine whether and how large "Gaps" are.

- Risk Assessment: The risk assessment should address the areas identified in the Gap analysis requiring remediation. A risk assessment should provide an analysis of both likely and unlikely scenarios in terms of probability of occurrence and their impact on the organization.

HIPAA does provide a "common sense" approach to implementing recommended and required security procedures. The list of tools and techniques to protect Web-applications include authentication, encryption, smart-cards or secure identification cards, and digital signatures.

Further, HIPAA mandates that security standards must be applied to preserve health information confidentiality and privacy in four main areas:

- Administrative Procedures: (personnel procedures, etc.)
- Physical Safeguards: (e.g., locks, etc.)
- Technical Security Services: To protect data at rest.
- Technical Security Mechanisms: To protect data in transit.

The security standard mandates safeguards for physical storage and maintenance, transmission, and access to individual health information. The standard also requires safeguards, such as encryption for Internet use as well as security mechanisms to guard against unauthorized access to data transmitted over a network. The recent incident at the University of Washington Medical

Center highlights the sensitivity as well as the vulnerability of health care data systems connected to the Internet to outside threats. A hacker called "Kane: managed to download admission records for four thousand heart patients in June/July 2000. The hospital would have faced stiff penalties if HIPAA had been enforced. As one can imagine, the risks to a healthcare provider of inadequate computer security could include harm to a patient, liability of leaked information, loss of reputation and market share, and fostering public mistrust of the technology. As a result of this breach of security, the University of Washington Medical Center recommended several precautionary steps to protect and secure PHI[10]:

1) Risk Analysis: Acknowledge potential vulnerabilities associated with both the internal or external process of storing, transmitting, handling, disseminating, communicating, and accessing PHI. Therefore each business unit should access potential vulnerabilities by

- Identifying and documenting all EPHI repositories
- Periodically re-inventory EPHI repositories

---

[10] WASHINGTON UNIVERSITY School of Medicine. HIPAA Security Policy #2, *"Administrative Safeguards for Security Management Policy"*. St. Louis. Jan 1, 2004

- Identifying the potential vulnerabilities to each repository
- Assigning a level of risk to each EPHI repository

All repositories of EPHI will be identified and logged into a common catalogue, in the appropriate medium form used, with the appropriate level of file, system, and owner information.

Some of the user/owner identifiers should include: Repository name, custodian name, custodian contact information, number of users that access the repository, number of records, system name, system IP address, system location, system manager and contact information. Further, each

Business Unit should update its EPHI inventory at least annually to ensure that the EPHI catalogue is up to date and accurate.

2) <u>Risk Management</u>: Each Business Unit must implement security measures and safeguards for each EPHI repository sufficient to reduce risks and vulnerabilities to a reasonable and appropriate level. The level, complexity and cost of such security measures and safeguards must be commensurate with the risk classification of each such EPHI repository. For example, low risk EPHI repositories may be appropriately safeguarded by normal best-practice security measures in place such as user accounts, passwords and perimeter firewalls. Medium and high- risk EPHI repositories must be secured in accordance with <u>HIPAA Security Policies #1-17.</u>

3) <u>Sanctions for Noncompliance</u>: Unfortunately, WU experienced a serious breach in the security of EPHI repositories and had to adopt sanctions for noncompliance to prevent both lawsuits and fines.

4) <u>Information System Activity Review</u>: It is imperative that internal audit procedures must be implemented to regularly review records of information system activity, such as audit logs, access reports, and security incident tracking reports. This is to ensure that system activity for all systems classified as medium and high risk is appropriately monitored and reviewed. Each

Business Unit should implement an internal audit procedure to regularly review records of system activity (examine audit logs, activity reports, or other mechanisms to document and manage system activity) every 90 days or less.

5) <u>HIPAA compliance/Risk Management officer</u>: Finally, all health care organizations should have a HIPAA compliance/Risk Management officer with proper training and credentials, such as Information Systems Security Professional (CISSP) and/or the Certified Information Systems

Auditor (CISA). This person should works closely with the Information Systems personnel and management to ensure compliance, continuity, conformity and consistency with the protection of PHI privacy and security[11].

Most important is to develop a corporate culture that communicates with all levels of the organization's workforce. This involves writing periodic reminders, providing in-services, and orienting new hires to the intent of the policies. All of these training activities must be conducted using easily understood terms and examples. Secondly, all of these standards should be a part of an organization's overall security strategy and are critical from a risk mitigation standpoint. Finally, PHI security needs to have the full support and cooperation from the executive level of the organization.

Help or Hindrance?

Increasingly sophisticated technology presents opportunities in advancing integrated healthcare. Clearly, automation and technology helps improve the access and quality of care, while reducing administrative costs. Unfortunately, when PHI information is shared both internally and externally by multiple users, a health care organization must put safeguards in place to prevent a compromise to the security of PHI by a disgruntle employee or outside "hacker".

---

[11] Dorsey, Amanda. HIPAA/SECURE: Security Q/A. "So, You need Security...". Phoenix Health Systems, August 2004.

Positive Aspects of HIPAA. There are many positive aspects that have come from the legislation of the act. The first being a standardization of identifiers that make it possible to communicate effectively, efficiently and consistently with regards to PHI. Whether it is the pharmacist, doctor, hospital, insurance company or TPA, the standardization of electronic PHI data helps in the access and dissemination of data needed to process claims and deliver healthcare effectively. Thus, efficiencies have been gained, in this respect, as a result of HIPAA compliance.

A second benefit is that it has made the health care provider/insurance related industry more cognizant of associated risks related to the storage, access and retrieval of sensitive PHI.

Doctor's offices, hospitals, and ancillary providers have had a primary focus on treating the patient at hand. Organization of medical data that included sensitive PHI is a necessary bi- product of the paperwork that it generates. Prior to HIPAA, physical patient files were stored on the walls, halls, or periphery of the practice without much thought to exposure of sensitive PHI. Electronically stored PHI was handled in a similar haphazard manner. In the past, I have personally experienced exposed patient files as I walked down the hall of a doctor's office wondering that even the janitor had just as much access to sensitive PHI data as the physician. Because of this mandatory HIPAA compliance for safe storage, retrieval and transmission of physical and electronic PHI, it has led to a "best practice" standard for the responsibilities associated with PHI. Further, this increased awareness promotes a secure feeling for the patient that the provider/insurance company is making a conscious effort to protect the privacy of such sensitive PHI.

A third benefit is the accountability through the use of monitoring and updating the security aspect of PHI. HIPAA demands an ongoing effort to make sure PHI privacy and security is maintained and protected. This can ensure that sensitive PHI will have a lesser chance of being compromised.

The final benefit is that of disaster planning. 9/11 in conjunction with HIPAA mandates have made all health care providers and associated industries acutely aware of business continuity in the event of disaster. A patient may need to be seen suddenly at a hospital in a disaster zone that requires specific PHI and patient data that has been stored on an electronic file. Having backup/recovery systems can help in the continuity and quality of health care delivery for any patient.

Negative Aspects of HIPAA. HIPAA has some serious residual negative challenges as health care providers and insurance related industries become compliant to the Act. The first is cost. Since April 14, 2003, when the privacy rule of the Health Insurance Portability and Accountability Act took effect, health-care organizations have spent years and well over $17 billion dollars in an effort to comply with HIPAA[12]. The additional cost of a security compliance officer in larger organizations, the cost related to training all employees and making sure both the physical facilities as well as the maintenance and integrity of IT systems create a drain on cash flow and help to decrease profitability.

Complications of interpretation and compliance are another negative aspect that the Act imposes on the health care industry. Clearly, meeting HIPAA mandates is a complex and arduous task.

The security standard was developed with the intent of remaining technologically neutral in order to facilitate adoption of the latest and most promising developments in evolving technology and to meet the needs of healthcare entities of different size and complexity. As previously stated, the Health Insurance Portability and Accountability Act was passed with provisions subtitled Administrative Simplification. It appears to be anything but simple. Instead, the standard is a compendium of security requirements that must be satisfied. The problem is how the law will be applied from provider to provider in a compliant manner. Regardless of the difficulty, each provider must meet the basic requirements. A concern expressed by healthcare providers and administrators, besides cost, is how to address all or some of the standards, especially when compliance requirements are vague (Bogen, 2001).

Fines and Penalties are another still negative by-product of the Act those who do not comply will experience. Some companies, whether by cost prohibition, ignorance or defiance, are choosing not to be HIPAA

---

[12] Scheffenacke, E.B."HIPAA: Bad Law or Bad Press"

compliant. Attorneys nationwide reportedly plan to deploy decoy patients at health care organizations to see if doctors, dentists, hospitals and insurance companies have the policies, procedures and protections that ensure patients' privacy, as required by the federal Health Insurance Portability and Accountability Act (HIPAA). Those that do not comply risk hefty fines, possible criminal prosecution and costly civil lawsuits. Companies have had two years to educate staff, designate a privacy officer and adopt basic security measures[13]. The U.S. department of Health Human Services' Office of Civil Rights will have the authority to investigate suspected offenders, namely purported victims who slap health care providers with big-money lawsuits. The threat of lawsuits may be a stronger motivator than government fines or jail time. Like it or not, by 2005, the recently approved HIPAA security regulations will become enforceable. By then, all health care organizations, and their associated venders, must have a security program that includes security awareness training, risk assessments and disaster recovery plans.

A fourth negative by-product of the Act is loss of productivity. Insurance companies, prior to HIPAA, were for the most part fairly compliant as proprietary safe guards under physical constraints protected much of the PHI kept in repositories. Doctors, dentists and hospitals on the other hand, had loose policy and procedures regarding the protection and security of PHI. This is primarily because these frontline health care providers are more concerned with treating the patient than the details and business of record keeping. Many of these frontline health care providers are now spending more time and resources in the area of lost productivity regarding patient care delivery by trying to be HIPAA compliant.

---

[13] Saita, Anne. "HIPAA Prescribes Privacy Regimen" www.infosecuritymag.techtarget.com

Conclusion

In the era of managed care and thin financial margins, the competitiveness of providers will depend on the use of information technology to streamline clinical and other business operations. Much of this will require the transmission of PHI through various communication mediums. Therefore, it is crucial how this PHI is handled, disseminated, communicated and accessed by health care organizations. Increased computerization of medical information requires increased surveillance of policies and procedures to protect the confidentiality of private medical data. Failure to develop, implement, audit, and document information security procedures could result in serious consequences, such as penalties and loss of reputations, market share, and patient trust.

The government has publicly stated it will be very forgiving if an organization demonstrates it meant well and has taken steps to become compliant. Some measures recommended by HIPAA experts are minor in expense, but go a long way toward showing an earnest effort. For instance, be sure that computers storing or displaying sensitive PHI records automatically log off or lock up after use to prevent any unauthorized access. Also, organizations should establish policies for shredding documents, locking file cabinets and playing white noise or music to inhibit eavesdropping. Each HIPAA-regulated organization also should have a privacy officer to make sure the staff understands and follows HIPAA guidelines.

Finally, as to whether or not HIPAA is helpful or a hindrance, I believe it comes as mixed blessing. No matter how much effort we put into PHI security and protection, bad guys still break into banks. The only thing we can do is take precautionary measures that make compromising the security of PHI difficult. The good aspects of the Act have improved standardization and efficiency. Further, it has developed a common protective culture and awareness, for those health care organizations that are making the effort to comply, that privacy and security of a patient's PHI must be vigilantly maintained. Unfortunately, those of us involved with patient care delivery and related services must recognize that this will incur additional cost, redirection of resources and the loss of productivity in the protection and security of PHI. It is the cost of doing business.

11. Case. Network Doctors[*]

The Basics

The consulting agency known as 'Networking Doctors' has been asked to submit a proposal to supply a highly secure networking solution to the medical firm of Jordan, Mirchandani, and Singh. Peter Parker had joined 'Networking Doctors' in the summer of 2000 after graduating with a Bachelor of Science in Information Systems at George Mason University. He has been assigned this particular project. The firm's offices will be located in Henrico county Virginia, in a building that is approximately 70 years old. The building has been used as a medical practice for the past 30 years, so no internal structural changes have been planned. However, the new occupants of the facility wish to bring the practice into the 21st century and want to outfit the building with all of the necessary computers and networking infrastructure to run a modern day medical practice. The firm

---

[*] This case was prepared by Soni Vaswani under the tutelage od Dr. Gurpreet Dhillon, Virginia Commonwealth University

has used the business requirements, based on the conditions of satisfaction, that were gathered from interviews with Dr. Singh, Dr. Mirchandani, Dr. Jordan and their office manager Mr. Pete Sampras in order to construct the proposal.

Based on several findings, Mr. Parker believes that a wireless network would best meet the firm's needs. Therefore; he plans to implement it using the 802.11g standard and all Linksys hardware. As per Dr. Satish Mirchandani's request he has included a detailed listing of the hardware and security software that he believes is needed in order to get the office up and running.

This case analysis report includes the following:

1. The business requirements that were provided by the firm's partners.

2. The proposed solution.

3. A listing of how the solution meets each of the business requirements.

4. A mockup of the building layout that displays the location for the proposed network components (and other hardware such as printers, personal computers, and the file server).

5. A detailed technical description of the various pieces of hardware.

6. Wireless Networking Standards (a high-level comparison) 802.11a, 802.11b and 802.11g.

7. Wireless Network Security (WEP, Firewalls and VPN's) the solution addresses the issue.

8. A price breakdown structure that denotes the turnkey price for each component (includes configuration and implementation).

The Business Requirements ██████████████████████

Each business requirement corresponds directly to a condition of satisfaction stated by the customer.

BR1-Security. The practice needs to set security standards and guidelines which protect clear instruction to protect the entity's information, processing platforms, and network.

BR2-Freedom of movement. The practice needs to be able to implement a solution that will allow the healthcare providers the ability to move though out the facility and have patient's information readily available to them on demand.

BR3-Low maintenance and dependable. The practice needs to be able to implement a solution that will require a relatively low degree of maintenance. The network and hardware solutions should not sacrifice dependability for unnecessary functionality (bells and whistles).

BR4-Eliminate unnecessary paper document management. The practice needs to implement a solution that will allow the healthcare providers to manage their patient's information in an environment that will only require the maintenance and storage of essential paper documents. All other documents and charts will be accessed, maintained and stored electronically.

BR5-Ability to use existing application software. The practice needs to employ a solution that will not require a change in the current patient management or financial accounting software.

BR6-Appropriate response time. The practice needs to provide a solution that will allow the healthcare provider to access needed information in a timely manner.

BR7-Scaleability. The practice needs to implement a solution that will support the current number of users and that will scale appropriately if the number of users should increase.

BR8- Portability. The practice requires that the three physicians should be able to take their personal computing devices with them when they are working outside of the practice facility located on Patterson Avenue.

BR9-Ease of use. The practice needs to employ a solution that will require more then a few hours training to allow the staff to continue performing their primary job functionalities.

BR10-Limit disruption to practice. The practice requires that the implementation of the networking solution have a limited amount of disruption to the daily operations of the practice.

BR11-Adhering to HIPAA. The practice needs to employ a solution that adheres to all of the technology constraints imposed by HIPAA

The Proposed Solution

Based on the business requirements noted above Peter proposes that a wireless networking solution be implemented. He will implement a solution that uses only Linksys® hardware for wireless communication. He also proposes the purchase of 3 Tablet style PCs, five workstations, five printers, and one file server. The proposal contains sections that cover the following; how a wireless solution addresses each of the business requirements, a technical description of the hardware recommended and the cost of each components, why his analysts chose to use the 802.11g standard over either 802.11a or 802.11b, how the plan to address the issues of security (Firewalls, Virus Protection and Virtual Private Networks), and a high level work breakdown structure depicting the anticipated project start and completion dates.

How the wireless solution addresses the business requirements:

BR-1 Security

A wireless network will create an approach which addresses confidentiality, availability, and integrity. The security program developed through the wireless network will consider all state, federal, and international level laws and regulations.

BR-2 Freedom of Movement

A wireless networking solution will facilitate the healthcare practitioner's freedom of movement if it is used in conjunction with a device such as a laptop or tablet PC that contains a wireless network card.

BR-3 Low Maintenance and Dependability

'Networking Doctors' have implemented or configured more than 20 wireless solutions in the greater Richmond metropolitan area and these solutions have proven to be just as dependable as any wired solution without any additional maintenance time or cost.

BR-4 Eliminate unnecessary paper document maintenance

Since patient information can be accessed anywhere in the facility with the proper authorization, there is no longer a need to lug around patient records and charts. A wireless network will allow the healthcare provider the same access that he or she had when sitting at his or her desk.

BR-5 Ability to use existing application software

Wireless devices can run in conjunction with any of the recent Microsoft and Apple operating systems and do not require the introduction of any obsolete software that may prohibit the use of any current mainstream applications.

BR-6 Appropriate response time

Although there may be a modest degradation in access times with a wireless network as opposed to a wired network the variance is so slight that it is virtually unnoticeable. However it must be stated that certain wireless devices may suffer interference from certain wireless phones and microwave ovens. This is a concern that will be addressed during system configuration

BR-7 Scalability

The wireless network configuration that Peter proposed will easily scale inline with the practices proposed business growth of one primary healthcare provider, two office personnel, and two nurses every two years.

BR-8 Portability

The wireless solution will allow the primary healthcare providers to roam anywhere within the confines of the building and access needed information. The network solution will also allow physicians to access information contained on their internal network securely any where in the world through the use of a VPN (Virtual Private Network).

BR-9 Ease of use

The introduction of the Tablet PC will allow the primary healthcare providers to enter information into their applications through the uses of a stylist. This will more closely resemble taking notes using free hand as opposed to having to use the defined number and lettering formats required by PDA's. The introduction of the wireless network should have discernible impact on individuals performing there job other then the increased mobility associated with being "unbound".

BR-10 Limit disruption to practice

The actual implementation and configuration of the wireless network is very non-invasive. The wireless devices require a minimal number of wires to run between them and the actual machines (PC's, printers, etc.) therefore there is almost never a need to "pull cable" between rooms or floors and most devices can be installed with a drill, hammer and a screwdriver causing very little if any mess at all.

BR-11 Adhering to HIPAA

Based on Peter's understanding of the HIPAA computing and security requirements the wireless solution will be 100% compliant.

Physical Design

Information security is very important within the medical industry. In fact, over the years, this market has even formed its own distinct niche in the world of information systems development. The information contained in medical information systems is very personal, and if unwanted third parties gained access to this information, not only would it be a major violation of doctor – patient privilege, but it could also cost these patients thousands of dollars at the very least. For this reason, certain practices must be undertaken to keep medical information secure.

There are a variety of people and organizations who would value information about peoples' health and medical history. Medical insurance companies and HMOs would like this information because they could use this information to raise the rates of people they insure. They could also refuse to grant a policy to people who they think would cost too much to insure. Companies hiring new employees could also be interested in their potential employees' medical records. The records might show they have a history of missing large amounts of time at work for medical reasons. These companies might also want to know about potential employees' family members who would fall under that company's group medical insurance rates. If the company is small, this could raise the insurance rates for everybody under that company's group insurance policy. Hiring companies' access to medical information could also hurt the employment chances of less healthy potential employees. Drug companies would also like this information so they can market their products better. Mortgage lenders might also be interested in peoples' health records to make sure they will live long enough and remain healthy enough to pay off their loans. Beyond this, any individual with intent to harm could use this personal information against their target.

While there are many illegitimate (even illegal) uses for peoples' medical histories, there are also a number of justifiable uses. If one patient visits his or her primary care physician, that patient could have a file containing his or her medical history at that doctor's office. Many things become possible if this file is stored electronically. If the primary care physician refers the patient to a specialist, this file could easily be transferred to the new doctor. If the patient must go to the hospital, the records could easily be transferred to the hospital the patent check in to. The local hospital could even hold a copy of the patients' records as a precautionary measure. That way, if the patient must visit the hospital's emergency room, no time will be wasted transferring medical data since it is already at the hospital. The fast, easy accessibility of this information could even save lives. Furthermore, if patients are away from home and they must visit a doctor, that doctor could obtain the medical records of patients more easily. Even drug stores could access some of this information to get patients' prescriptions ready faster.

In short, if patients' medical histories are stored and transferred electronically, it can lead to faster, more efficient, more thorough medical treatment.

The health care industry can make heavy use of wireless networks.

One reason for this is the nature of doctors' work environments. The proverbial doctor's office is not merely one room in one building; it is now several rooms throughout a building, or one room in each of several buildings, or even an array of rooms scattered throughout many buildings. As many professions require these days, doctors must access computers to do their work. However, if they only have one computer in one location, this could make accessing the computer and the information on it terribly inefficient, even in the smallest practice. The logical solution to this problem is to implement wireless networks in doctors' offices and hospitals. Once these are in place, doctors can easily carry laptops, tablet PCs and PDAs from room to room, allowing them to access their data efficiently. In some instances, doctors' offices and hospitals may even want to take it a step further and implement Bluetooth networks or some other type of personal area network (PAN). If this is done, a doctor could enter a room with a patient in it and that patient's medical data immediately comes onto the screen of his computing device. This could change health care, but there is some risk. The risk involved with wireless networks stemming from information security issues keeps medical practices large and small from implementing wireless networks for this purpose on a widespread scale.

Regardless of the hardware used to access a wireless network, there are a variety of risks any such network faces. These can be grouped into seven categories: insertion attacks, jamming, interception and unauthorized monitoring of wireless network traffic, client to client attacks, encryption attacks, brute force attacks against access point passwords, and misconfigurations. Insertion attacks occur when unauthorized devices are deployed on the wireless network or when new networks are created without the proper security features and protocols. This would include the "war drivers" and those who access wireless LANs via rogue access points. These rogue access points are frequently the points of origin for other attacks, including virus attacks (www.documents.iss.net). This is how viruses often enter networks. Fortunately, they can be guarded against similarly to how PCs defend themselves against viruses. For example, McAfee offers a package called 'VirusScan Wireless' that incorporates traditional antivirus software geared for a network with some of the security features of a firewall (Walters, 2003). Monitoring network traffic can be particularly damaging to a network's security. The reason for this is that by using wireless packet analysis, a hacker can look at the header attached to any packet traveling over the network, and since the header contains the username and password, he would have easy access to this information. Once a hacker has a username and password, he can use that information to bypass security features or pose as an authorized user on the network. Through jamming and client to client attacks, hackers can flood the frequency a wireless network operates on, creating denial of service problems for legitimate users on a network. Encryption attacks can occur because 802.11b's built in encryption, wireless equivalent privacy (WEP), has known weaknesses that attackers can exploit. Brute force attacks are generally caused by attackers trying to guess every possible password. Most problems stemming from misconfiguration are due to the way wireless packages are often bundled; they are initially configured for ease of use, not for network security. Settings must be changed to ensure network integrity (www.documents.iss.net). Some of these concerns can be addressed by network administrators. Others are present due to the nature of network hardware or the protocols and standards governing wireless LANs. To make a network containing sensitive medical data, one must address as many security concerns as possible, particularly those caused by unauthorized access and the damage caused by those who access a network in this manner.

The threat posed by unauthorized access to medical information over wireless networks can actually be broken down into two separate risks (www2.sis.pitt.edu). One risk is people simply gaining access to and viewing data they have no business viewing. However, a more dangerous threat comes from those who may access the medical records of individuals and then change them. While the number of those interested in changing the medical records of patients would be smaller than the number of those interested in viewing them, this group could do much more damage. Whereas those interested in only viewing the records could deny patient's health insurance or a new job, among other things, those interested in changing the records could cost patients their lives. While this is a worst case scenario, unauthorized changes made to medical records can certainly lead to inaccurate or incomplete medical records. Individuals may want to erase items from their medical history to appear as a lower health risk when applying for health insurance. If these systems are connected to the hospital's billing system, they may want to take things off their hospital bill. To prevent unauthorized access to these systems and the information they contain, hospitals and doctors' offices must undertake new security procedures.

Wireless networks open up a world of possibilities for medical institutions, but they are inherently not as safe as land based networks. According to a recent survey, 90% of those polled were "very concerned" or "somewhat concerned" about the security of wireless networks (infosecuritymag.techtarget.com). Anyone within a short enough distance from the antenna would have access to the network. One type of hacker known as a "war driver" drives around cities looking for wireless networks to get on (www.msnbc.com). Beyond people hacking wireless networks from their cars, some buy or even make antennas to access wireless networks up to 2,000 feet away (www.computerworld.com). In contrast, most 802.11b wireless networks can only be accessed by those within about 300 feet of a wireless access point (documents.iss.net). They are not hard to find; furthermore, not all of these networks are secure. Once an unauthorized user in on such a network, they can view or damage confidential information. Network administrators for wireless networks have several weapons with which to combat intrusions by hackers and other unauthorized users. For example, they can install firewalls and use encryption.

There are several possible points of attack for those interested in gaining unauthorized access to wireless networks. The first such point is at the end nodes on the networks. Not all of the end points on wireless networks were installed by IT departments. Employees sometimes add devices of their own to the networks. While these, by themselves, are not usually a major threat to network security, they do make unauthorized access points more difficult to find. In fact, Thor Sigvaldson, director of the advanced technology group at PricewaterhouseCoopers Consulting, estimates that every company, branch office or store with over 50 employees has at least one unauthorized "rogue" access point (www.computerworld.com). While this is a problem, companies and organizations with wireless networks can use a variety of software packages by several different vendors to detect and locate all access points on the network. Other software packages, such as IBM's Wireless Security Auditor, make it possible to find and identify potential areas where perpetrators may gain unauthorized access to wireless networks (www.wi-fiplanet.com).

There are many more security concerns involving wireless LANs. PDAs and other handheld devices are not designed for, and often are not capable of supporting the proper security measures to ensure the integrity of the network and the information on it. Furthermore, these devices are often small can easy be stolen, creating another threat to security. One other problem with these networks as they currently exist is the protocol they are running under. The majority of the wireless LANs today are running IEEE standard 802.11, which is simply inadequate for anything but the simplest security procedures. These include authentication and basic access control. Also, 802.11b's built-in encryption has shown itself to be limited and easy to break (www.infosecuritymag.techtarget.com). Beyond this, wireless LANs conforming to IEEE standard 802.11 operate at the same frequency as cordless phones, Bluetooth PANs and household signal-emitting devices such as baby monitors. Because of this, the signals sent by these other devices interfere with those of wireless LANs (documents.iss.net).

Handheld devices, including PDAs, could be some of the biggest security risks to wireless networks. The reason for this is simple. Many of these devices started out merely as personal organizers. As time passed, they evolved into electronics with internet (and network) connectivity. Since this was an added feature, the designers considered security an afterthought; it also didn't hurt that these devices had a small amount of memory in which to install meaningful security features. As a result, they do don't have enough memory for solid password protection, encryption, and proper memory management. To illustrate some security problems with handheld devices, examine the Palm OS. It is unable to control a program's access to system resources. In addition, PDA passwords are not secure. Passwords used on Palm OS are encrypted and stored and are accessible by any application. Since the encryption is relatively weak, unauthorized users could easily determine the password and access the entire network. With all this in mind, the security features built into Palm handhelds are generally weaker than the similar features built into Microsoft and Texas Instruments products. Several companies, including RSA Security, Certicom and NTR, offer encryption solutions to makers of handheld devices. Also, a doctor with offices in several locations including a hospital may want to examine the possibility of installing a virtual private network (VPN). These can offer many of the features of a wireless LAN but without as many problems with encryption and authentication (www.infosecuritymag.techtarget.com).

Despite the numerous security concerns to wireless LANs, there are solutions available. As previously mentioned, there are antivirus programs designed to protect wireless networks. In addition, organizations installing wireless networks can also hire security consultants to help ensure the integrity of their network. Network administrators for wireless LANs can implement firewalls on their networks. Not only will these make it tougher for outside users to access the network, but they can also make traffic within the network more efficient. It is this functionality that would make the firewall effective when used on a wireless network. A network administrator can set up filters and flags in an application gateway that could detect when those on the network attempt to access information they should not be viewing (Tanenbaum, 2003). Another technology that can be used to protect wireless networks is spread spectrum. Using this, the data transferred is sent on multiple changing frequencies, making it harder for unauthorized users to get the whole message being sent. Spread spectrum in an effective tool in reducing the risk of eavesdropping and interference of a wireless LAN (Nichols and Lekkas, 2003).

Lifespan, a health network in Rhode Island, manages patient care and administrative services at four hospitals in that state. At these four hospitals, doctors and other employees can use the wireless networks in place to access patient records and issue care instructions. The wireless LANs have worked well for the Lifespan hospitals; they plan on extending their use into the hospitals' operating rooms. Lifespan Chief Technology Officer David Hemendinger says that the wireless LANs reduce paperwork, save time, and aid in decision making (Ellison, 2003). Doctors Jordan, Mirchandani and Singh could employ wireless LANs in much the same way that Lifespan did, but on a smaller scale. They could access information from anywhere in their office and not be limited to looking at a computer screen in a fixed location. As for accessing the network while at any hospital, one option would be to use VPNs.

Equipment requirements

- Wireless hardware components
- Wireless Signal Booster
- Wireless Bridge
- Wireless Print Server
- Wireless PC network card
- Wireless Notebook Adapter
- File Server
- Tablet PC
- Workstations
- Network Printer
- Uninterrupted Power Supply
- Firewall and Anti Virus Software

Peter and his consultants need to keep in mind the following aspects when setting up and using the wireless network.

1.   Performance

The actual performance of a wireless network depends on a number of factors, including:

- In an Infrastructure environment, one's distance from the access point. As you get farther away, the transmission speed will decrease.

- Structural interference. The shape of the building or structure, the type of construction, and the building materials used may have an adverse impact on signal quality and speed.

- The placement and orientation of the wireless devices.

2. Interference.

Any device operating in the 2.4 GHz spectrum may cause network interference with a 802.11b wireless device. Some devices that may prove troublesome include 2.4 GHz cordless phones, microwave ovens, adjacent public hotspots, and neighboring 802.11b wireless LANs.

3. Security.

The current generation of Linksys products provide several network security features; and they require the following tasks to be performed by the end-user for successful implementation.

While the following is a complete list, steps A through E would be followed:

- Change the default SSID.
- Disable SSID Broadcasts.
- Change the default password for the Administrator account.
- Enable MAC Address Filtering.
- Change the SSID periodically.
- Enable WEP 128-bit Encryption. Please note that this will reduce your network performance.
- Change the WEP encryption keys periodically.

4. Security Threats Facing Wireless Networks

Wireless networks are easy to find. Hackers know that in order to join a wireless network, wireless networking products first listen for "beacon messages". These messages are unencrypted and contain much of the network's information, such as the network's SSID (Service Set Identifier) and the IP Address of the network PC or access point. One result of this, seen in many large cities and business districts, is called "Warchalking". This is one of the terms used for hackers looking to access free bandwidth and free Internet access through the wireless network. These are the steps Peter can take to prevent any such threats:

Change the administrator's password regularly. With every wireless networking device used, Peter should keep in mind that network settings (SSID, WEP keys, etc.) are stored in its firmware. The network administrator is the only person who can change network settings. If a hacker gets a hold of the administrator's password, he, too, can change those settings. So one would need to make it harder for a hacker to get that information. Change the administrator's password regularly.

SSID. There are several things to keep in mind about the SSID:

- Disable Broadcast
- Make it unique.
- Change it often

Most wireless networking devices will give Peter the option of broadcasting the SSID. While this option may be more convenient, it allows anyone to log into a wireless network. This includes hackers. The SSID is never broadcasted.

Wireless networking products come with a default SSID set by the factory. Hackers know these defaults and can check these against a specific network. The SSID is changed to something unique and not something related to the company or the networking products used.

MAC Addresses. It is crucial to enable MAC Address filtering. MAC Address filtering will allow Peter to provide access to only those wireless nodes with certain MAC Addresses. This makes it harder for a hacker to access the network with a random MAC Address.

WEP Encryption. Wired Equivalent Privacy (WEP) is often looked upon as a panacea for wireless security concerns. This is overstating WEP's ability. Again, this can only provide enough security to make a hacker's job more difficult.

There are several ways that WEP can be maximized:

- Use the highest level of encryption possible
- Use a "Shared" Key
- Use multiple WEP keys
- Change the WEP key regularly

Implementing encryption will have a negative impact on the network's performance. If the doctors choose to transmit sensitive data over the network, encryption should be used.

Practice

When a physician chooses to send electronic order forms from personal computers at remote offices and in their homes the need for virtual private network technology develops. VPNs create secure connections between internal networks and remote PCs. The data transferred is scrambled via encryption applications. The three doctors have a choice of using the World Wide Web for browser based remote access or the conventional IPsec VPN method. Netilla Networks, based in Somerset, NJ, provides VPN technology that uses a secure socket layer, or SSL, 128-bit encryption which has become the standard for browser security. Using a web-based vpn certainly has it's plus and minus points. The alternative conventional VPN uses IP security protocol, or IPsec, to create dedicated modem-to-modem connections to internal networks via standard desktop interfaces. This technology has been the traditional form of VPN used for years and allows IT staff to remotely troubleshoot network problems and perform routine maintenance. However, the use of IPsec VPN is not compatible with today's remote access initiatives. Maintenance costs are quite high since each connection requires a separate phone line and large, complex software packages for installation which can only be implemented by I.T. staff. IPsec-based VPNs are configured to provide "network level" access to an internal network and this enables the end user to easily navigate through the guts of the network's infrastructure. On the other hand, SSL-based VPNs also require software to be loaded on a remote computer. Yet the "footprint" of the software is much smaller and the application can be downloaded through a website and automatically loaded. Eliminating an on-site technician visit saves time. Unlike IPsec VPNs, the web-based technology is not limited to slow dial-up modem connections. It is absolutely crucial that the software be configured properly and implemented with the right policies and procedures. Not doing so will result in a security risk. SSL-based VPNs are quite common and they allow organizations to create "application-level" access to their internal networks. In other words, the package can be used to set up remote access only to specific applications. In comparison, the conventional IPsec VPNs provide much network level access. Basically once a user has established a successful VPN connection, their browser displays links to only the applications they're authorized to see. The IPsec connection is less discrete than the SSL-based option. The VPN connection which does not need additional software on a workstation is referred to as "clientless". In this case, a physician can use any computer with a Web browser to create a VPN tunnel. He or she would need to login with a user id and a password. Many health care organizations are not completely comfortable with implementing the clientless version. The biggest reason for this decision is they want to maintain a certain amount of control while providing remote access. This can known as "managed" VPN. Security is easily managed because the delivery system knows something about each remote client connected to it's network. One of the common limitations posed by a managed VPN connection is the lack of a single sign-on process. If a user has to access to five different applications while using a virtual private network, the user must enter a separate username and password for each program. On the same token, they cannot have more than one application open simultaneously. If a doctor wants to enter the same information about a patient on several different screens, they must log in and out of each application. This may or may not be a complaint for one of the three doctors.

One other topic of concern for health care officials who are considering Internet-based VPNs is the security problem caused by split tunneling. Split tunneling occurs when remote users are simultaneously connected to the public Internet and a private internal network. Most of the time this occurs when an end user has established a successful VPN connection and then decides to access a website to check email, purchase email, or even trade stocks online. Split tunneling poses to be an issue because it opens up a security hole for a virus or other harmful code. The virus could infect the remote pc and use the VPN connection as a conduit into the private network. Therefore; it is absolutely important remote workstations be configured properly and have the appropriate protection, such as anti-virus programs and firewalls. VPN implementation requires absolute attention to proper installation and the commitment to follow the policies and procedures. The HIPAA (Health Insurance Portability and Accountability Act) specifically requires hospitals to be responsible for users who are accessing protected health information. Unfortunately many organizations don't require remote users to install firewalls or update virus protection programs on their pcs. On the other hand, certain companies create agreements which allow I.T. staff to visit remote locations (such as a user's home) and ensure procedures are followed. This practice has not yet started occurring in health care (Gillespie, 2003).

Certain secure websites provide remote access to patient records. This is possible with the use of a program called the Physician Portal. For example a doctor can log onto one of the secure sites that puts patient charts, lab results, transcribed reports, and nurses' notes all at his or her fingertips. This helps the doctors know what kind of work and how much is waiting for them before they arrive at the hospital. The doctors could use such a system to help organize their day better. To access the portal from a remote location, the doctors use a "key fob". The device is attached to a key chain and displays a different number every 30 seconds. A physician would have to type in that number along with a pin to access the system. Dr. Dennis A. Ehrich, a cardiologist with Cardiovascular Group of Syracuse, believes this technology will improve the quality of health care. He suggests this will reduce the rate of medical errors and prevent near mishaps in treatment because one can instantaneously access laboratory data (Mulder, 2003).

The devices needed to access a VPN can range from a 'key fob' to 'smart card'. If the doctors choose to try this product they would not be making a bad decision. Gemplus International S.A. is the world's leading provider of smart card solutions. The cards they provide allow employees to securely access patient information across the health care network. The smart cards can be integrated to utilize Active Directory certificates to provide a single sign-on solution. The implementation is cost effective can be completed within three weeks. The usage of these cards complies with HIPAA regulations and the single sign-on eliminates the security risk of employees sharing passwords protecting sensitive patient information from unauthorized access. The two-factor authentication combines the traditional "something you know" such as a password, with "something you have" such as the badge or card. This provides far greater security than the usual username and password. The unique authentication capabilities provide strong protection of confidential information, which is a top concern for hospitals as they work to streamline and secure medical data exchange (PR Newswire Europe, 2003).

Searching for the most suitable solution for the implementation of remote access does not have to be a difficult task for the doctors. If they decide to consider the other alternatives to the Linksys products, Multi-Tech Systems and Southern Business Solutions (based in Cumming, Georgia) provides an inexpensive Multi-Tech SOHO RouteFinder VPN solution to provide secure remote access to patient data for both the physicians and staff. The Multi-Tech SOHO RouteFinder RF550VPN has an estimated price of $200. With use of the router, patient medical records can be accessed off-site. While offsite if an on-call physician needs to make a medical decision for a patient another doctor has already seen, he or she does not have to call the other provider for patient information. Normally physicians end up spending much time at the office finishing up charting duties. The router provides a solution which can allow them to tie into their electronic medical application from home. The router can be installed at the doctor's office and SSH Sentinel IPSec client software at the other remote sites. The RouteFinder is connected to the Internet via a DSL line and remote clients can also utilize DSL or dial-up lines to access the web while keeping up with a fast seamless connection. With this particular VPN solution, a physician can dial-in to the main office to securely access patient medical records and history and previous prescriptions. If there are any questions when one doctor is covering a colleague's patients or if a hospital ER calls, the attendees can promptly advise on medications, treatments, allergies as such. In addition, each conversation can be documented into the EMR immediately. Those who have access to the VPN can dial-in and connect directly to their desktops from home. In case of inclement weather, the scheduling staff will be able to pull up the scheduling application, call patients and reschedule appointments for a later time. The time frame needed for the rollout is quite feasible. It takes less than three hours to get the RouteFinder RF550VPN up and running at the server site and about an hour at each remote client. If the doctors were to select this product, SBS (Southern Business Solutions) could readily support the system after implementation. A tech could utilize the connection to securely dial-in to the customer's server in order to troubleshoot network problems, provide maintenance, and check back-up operations. Upgrades can be done after hours to minimize downtime for the practice (PR Newswire, 2003).

As far as the concept of scheduling appointments remotely is concerned, the doctors do not only have to rely on the RouteFinder product previously mentioned. One of the products offered by vpn technology is an Internet based case management and appointment scheduling system. 'E-Ceptionist' allows hospitals in a variety of areas to schedule consultations and manage the transfer of electronic patient records. The Italian Cardiology network known as 'Cardnet' has been added as one of the recent customers. The implementation of the service began about six months ago and Cardnet has already been reaping the many benefits of the system. (www.newsrx.com)

The growing use of remote and wireless networks by health care professionals presents much challenge to IT managers. One of the greatest ironies of the IT field is easier access relates to greater security risks. The ease of access that wireless and remote networks offer is matched by the security challenges presented by those networks. Decisions made about deployment of wireless local area networks (WLANs) must take into account the impact of the administrative pieces of the HIPAA. The privacy rules state a covered entity must have in place appropriate administrative, technical, and physical safeguards to protect privacy of electronic and nonelectronic protected health information. The HIPAA security rules were issued in final form on February 20, 2003. They apply to protected health information in electronic form only. The principles of the rules require covered entities to: "(1) ensure the confidentiality, integrity, and availability of all electronic protected health information the covered entity creates, receives, maintains, or transmits; (2) protect against any reasonably anticipated threats or hazards to the security or integrity of such information; (3) protect against any reasonably anticipated uses or disclosures of such information that are not permitted or required under [the security rules]; and (4) ensure compliance with the [security rules] by its workforce" (Gainer, 2003). The penalties for violating HIPAA laws range from one hundred dollars per person per incident to $250,000 and 10 years in prison for intentional violations. There is no doubt that the security rules affect how WLANs should be implemented. Several methods exist which could make a WLAN more secure. Covered health care entities generally have to decide whether they should postpone deploying an initial WLAN or upgrade WEP (Wireless Equivalent Privacy)-based WLAN, until planned changes in wireless network standards are adopted and have been implemented in commercial products. The folks in charge of maintaining security health care information systems have a lot to carry on their shoulders. As the world of technology changes constantly, those rules require covered entity managers and their respective lawyers to constantly evaluate the impact of the changes on the security of their networks.

Using VPN technology successfully and implementing the HIPAA laws requires much work and commitment. The Health Insurance Portability and Accountability Act of 1996 protects health insurance coverage for workers and their families when they change or lose their jobs. The HCFA (Health Care Financing Administration) governs the practices of HIPAA and requires strict encryption and authentication for transmitting privacy act information over the Internet. The HIPAA requires hospitals to be responsible for end users who are accessing protected health information. A cornerstone of the regulation is "minimum necessary data disclosure". In other words no one should see even one item of data more than he or she needs to do their job. The user profiles must not only be linked to screens and functions; they must be linked to specific data fields within the system (Korpman, 2002).

As the attention and awareness to HIPAA laws within health care increases, the industry is seeking ways in which to audit security of their networks. Qualys, Inc is a leading provider of on-demand security audit and vulnerability management solutions. They provide a service known as QualysGuard to regularly audit the security of their networks to protect patient info and hold onto a secure infrastructure. The doctors could use this process to comply with the complexities of the HIPAA. Qualys provides organizations with third-party capability to audit networks for vulnerabilities and fixes. The automated process reduces costs for network security audits. (www.newsrx.com)

Twelve

12. Case. DoubleClick*

The Basics

In recent years with the continued development of the new rough and wild American "Frontier," the Internet, we have experienced an entirely new development of uncharted legal questions and interpretations of the same old laws. Once thought to be a very black and white issue by the founding fathers in drafting the Constitution, an individual's right to privacy enters new interpretations as the Internet invades our homes and companies download and deposit information to and from our computers on a daily basis. The pivotal question is how far can these entities go in violating privacy and how much consent is necessary to allow them the free access they desire. The case of DoubleClick is one that exemplifies this development and demonstrates how a lack of attention to a clear and

* A version of this paper was also published in Journal of Information System Security, Volume 2, Issue 2 as "To opt-in, or to opt-out? That is the question. A Case Study," authored by Gurpreet Dhillon and Scott Chapman. Reproduced with permission from JISSec (www.jissec.org)

revealing strategy, taking into consideration all of the relevant factors of the environment, can almost be terminal to business. At the very least, it became a media and public image nightmare.

Company Background

Founded in 1995, DoubleClick began with its focus on "targeted" database marketing efforts utilizing direct advertising networks and technology to determine online users' patterns of Web surfing. Initially, DoubleClick was simply a "banner ad" company that tracked anonymous users when they chose directed banner ads and maintained data on those responses to better target advertisement. DoubleClick began providing this package of information as an enhanced marketing service to companies with an online presence allowing the companies to better understand the recipients of their ads. DoubleClick quickly progressed to one of the power-providers of online user profile information. DoubleClick's services stimulated tremendous growth and provided significant value for online companies contributing to DoubleClick's quick rise to success. DoubleClick combined technology, media and data expertise and centralized planning, execution, control, tracking and reporting for online media campaigns for their clients.

Headquartered in New York City with over 30 offices around the world, DoubleClick went public in February 1998 offering 3.5 million shares of stock, at $17.00 per share. Since that time, DoubleClick has embraced a strategy of acquisition and Information Technology development that has led to leaps of commercial successes mired by significant controversy.

By 1996, DoubleClick had been growing to quick success. Keven O'Conner, the founder and CEO of DoubleClick, stated in Forbes Magazine that DoubleClick's databases would never be connected to names and addresses and that matching of peoples private information "would be voluntary on the user's part, and used in strict confidence." He continued by stating, "We are not going to trick people or match information from other sources."

By 1999, DoubleClick had been taking aggressive moves to build their company and increase their ability to provide accurate and increasingly detailed information about online users. Essentially, they wanted to increase their already strong competitive advantage. DoubleClick felt that they had the IT ability to continue this competitive edge. In order to implement this strategy, DoubleClick merged with Abacus Direct, the nation's largest cataloging company that tracked the purchasing habits of catalog shoppers. Abacus' databases included more than 2 billion consumer catalog transactions with information on over 88 million American households, essentially 90% of the United States.

It soon became evident that DoubleClick's intention was to merge the Abacus database, which specifically contained the name and address information on purchasers, with DoubleClick's user databases to created a tremendous resources of online user information, destroying the anonymity aspect to the Internet. It appears though that with the acquisition of Abacus, DoubleCLick had reversed their initial strategy of protection and anonymity of the user.

Prior to the acquisition of Abacus, DoubleClick's revenues were based on targeting banner ads in less direct ways such as checking the Internet addresses of people who visit participating sites. This way, people in their homes or offices would see different ads as they browsed from different sites whether it was at work in a factory for General Motors, a machine shop in Ohio or at school in Nevada. Every time someone clicked on a DoubelClick client ad, DoubleClick would add that fact to its databases that were built from the cookies that it placed on users' hard drives. DoubleClick utilized the cookie technology to help them target the ads more precisely by understanding the habits of the user and compiling it into a user profile identified by an identification code.

Now, though, DoubleClick had undertaken a pursuit of a serious strategy to merge their own coded habit tracking information with the identity information of Abacus' databases. DoubleClick's advertising network would now correlate the names and addresses of Net shoppers of the Abacus Alliance database, made up of more than 2 billion consumer catalog transactions, with DoubleClick's consumer buying habits database, providing information about web customers that would allow marketers to send media ads to precisely the right targeted potential customer more efficiently. The idea was that DoubleClick would now be able to offer to its clients more directed and detailed information regarding the Web surfers that hit their sites.

That may not seem like that big of a deal. But, once the pervasive nature of each of the companies is understood, the ramifications quickly come into view and a massive and accurate database can visibly be developed. By 2000, DoubleClick had 1800 employees and over 7000 customers worldwide. DoubleClick was linked to over 11,500 web sites with over 50% of the Fortune 100 companies advertising on the DoubleClick network. Abacus, on the other hand, had information in its databases on 88 million households in the United States with over 90% of the household population in the database. The merger was a $1 billion deal.

The strategic decision to merge lead to serious public backlash and quickly revealed that DoubleClick's actions were not performed on sound ground. DoubleClick had always viewed this new information as simply an additional product that it would be able to offer its clients. Quickly, they realized that the public saw it as much more. The result of that strategy brought incredible consumer backlash and has even coined a term called "doubleclicking," when an entity attempts to track online surfing habits and invade privacy without consent, i.e. aggressive marketing. DoubleClick began to back-pedal through serious marketing efforts and image repair. The stock price was significantly affected while DoubleClick scrambled to repair its now tainted image. The stock price even suffered, from its opening at $17/share, it plummeted to $6 and $7/share.

To make matters worse, several lawsuits were filed by private citizens against DoubleClick for invasion of privacy, among other allegations. DoubleClick has been forced to defend those highly publicized cases. As well, several independent privacy protection groups filed complaints with federal administrative organizations, such at the Federal Trade Commission (FTC), complaining of violations of federal privacy statutes.

Certainly this was not the intent of DoubleClick when they embarked upon this strategy to merge and implement the IT solutions that they were developing. DoubleClick obviously knew that they would have been able to perform this type of merger of the databases and realized the potential commercial success that it could bring. However, DoubleClick seems to have not performed a thorough analysis of their strategy disregarding many factors, most importantly, the external environment.

The major events have played out as follows:

1995	- DoubleClick founded
2/20/98	- DoubleClick goes public
6/14/99	- DoubleClick announces merger with Abacus Direct
11/23/99	- Merger complete
12/99	- DoubleClick changes privacy policy
1/25/00	- USA Today reports that DoubleClick is going to "synchronizing" cookies with names and addresses
2/10/00	- EPIC files complaint with FTC
2/14/00	- DoubleClick announces changes to be made
3/2/00	- DoubleClick announces moratorium on attempts to merge names and cookie tracking devices
7/00	- FTC approves a set of industry principles for online advertising
1/22/01	- FTC closes investigation on the data-collection practices of DoubleClick finding no "unfair or deceptive" practices
1/2002	- Case proceeds to trial against DoubleClick for invasion of privacy filed by Hariet Judnick
April 2005	- Hellman & Friedman acquire DoubleClick and Abacus and operate as separate companies
Dec. 2006	- Abacus is sold to Epsilon Interactive
4/13/2007	- Google acquires DoubleClick for US$3.1 billion in cash

---

After the smoke continued to rise, Kevin O'Conner, the CEO of Doubleclick, issued a statement on March 2, 2000 informing the public that Doubleclick had not implemented its plan to merge the databases and that they had never associated names, or any other personally identifiable information, with anonymous user activity across Web sites. O'Conner continued that DoubleClick understands that the point of contention in the world regarding the Internet is "under what circumstances names can be associated with anonymous user activity across Web sites." He also stated that it was clear from discussions with hundreds of consumers, privacy advocates, customers, government officials and industry leaders that DoubleClick "made a mistake by planning to merge names with anonymous user activity across Web sites in the absence of government and industry privacy standards." So as a result, DoubleClick committed that until there was agreement between government and industry on privacy standards, DoubleClick would not link personally identifiable information to anonymous user activity across Web sites.

DoubleClick claimed that they had been very active in the online privacy issues with the FTC since 1997 and that they spent a lot of time on this in discussing the merger with Abacus. DoubleClick felt that if consumers were not happy, neither one of us would have much of a business. DoubleClick, as a result of this new commitment, had to place on hold a number of new products until they were able to identify industry or government standards, although, they did not change the core of the business.

With public sentiment growing against DoubleClick, they took extreme measures in trying to demonstrate their dedication to privacy, setting up a privacy panel, hiring a Chief Privacy Officer, establishing clear privacy policies and joining several corporate privacy protection groups. While these efforts have demonstrated significant improvement in public opinion and even quelled the storm created in the media, in the courts and in the FTC, this could have been avoided, had a significant strategic analysis been performed to determine whether this IT solution was in line with overall corporate policy and whether the IT solution would bring with it any other sort of negative ramification, whether external, internal, social, financial or governmental.

Arguments and Complaints

The key issue, with regard to the permissibility to track Internet users, really centers around the fact that being tracked doesn't live up to people's expectation of what they are getting while on the Internet, states Robert Smith, publisher of Privacy Journal. He continues, "They don't think that their physical locations, their names will be combined with what they do on the Internet. If they want to do that they have to expose that plan to the public and have it discussed." Tom Maddox of Privacy Place.com adds that this is very gnarly territory, this is the smoking gun, proof that privacy advocates warnings are not alarmist.

Complaints and Lawsuits

Embracing these opinions, Electronic Privacy Information Center (EPIC) and The Center for Democracy and Technology (CDT) filed a complaint with the FTC claiming unfair trade practices. These entities relied on the fact that DoubleClick had made past assurances that they would not collect any personal information on Internet users. The user would remain anonymous. EPIC also claimed that DoubleClick had failed to follow its revised privacy policy, which EPIC felt was also unfair as follows:

- Consumers are enrolled and tracked without their express permission;
- Consumers can't avoid the harm;
- The harm to privacy is not outweighed by countervailing benefits to consumers or competition;
- The Business model violates public policy.

In their complaint EPIC asked for relief in destruction of all records wrongfully obtained, assessment of civil penalties for the behavior and injunctive relief enjoining DoubleClick from violating the Federal Trade Commission Act. While the complaint was filed to essentially test the current state of privacy protection in the United States, accountability is hoped for as a result.

As mentioned, another party, Hariet Judnick, filed a lawsuit in Marin County, California, shortly thereafter, based on the argument that "the California constitution's right to privacy stands for the proposition that companies like DoubleClick have to seek permission before they track, store and analyze what families look at and click on, on the Internet. So it basically means that we believe the lawful model would be opt-in, not opt-out," according to her attorney, Ira Rothken, San Rafael, California. Similar cases were filed around the country.

The lawsuit alleges that DoubleClick "represented to the general public that it was not collecting personal and identifying information and that it gives privacy interests of Internet users" the utmost importance. It claims that DoubleClick combined the power of its cookie technology with the information it acquired to create a "sophisticated and highly intrusive means of collecting and cross referencing private personal information without the consent of Internet users." Judnick wanted an injunction against DoubleClick to stop it from using the technology and asked for a clear simple method by which Internet users can destroy collected private information. It also asked that DoubleClick be required to destroy all records obtained without customer knowing consent.

Mark Rotenberg from the EPIC says "what they are doing is simply wrong, that is why we've been trying to make the case against self regulation: These policies quickly collapse when an opportunity presents itself, and that is what we're seeing here."

In another realm of trouble, an independent group called JunkBusters forwarded letters to major Mutual and Stock Fund Managers requesting that they remove all companies from their portfolios that have demonstrated an unwillingness to protect the privacy of their customers through similar acts as DoubleClick.

"Opt-in" versus "Opt-out"

One of the pivotal issues of contention is that DoubleClick feels that the users should have to affirmatively choose that they do not want to be a part of the tracking and profiling, since the de-facto consent to invasion by being on the Internet. This is termed "opt-out." Conversely the opposition feels that the consumer should not be profiled until they have affirmatively chosen that they do want to be a part of the tracking and profiling. This is termed "opt-in." DoubleClick felt that they would give the consumers opt-out options and inform them of the disclosure policies that would assist them in understanding what is being done with their data.

DoubleClick's actions really appear disingenuous when the chance to opt out comes only in the form of a few lines of text placed in the privacy policies of participating Web sites. Since such policies are usually buried a few levels down, it's rare for the consumers to find out if personal information is being collected or their identity is being established, let alone them having a chance to opt out. David Banisar, Deputy Director of Privacy International feels like this is "fraudulent on its face."

Interestingly enough the attorney for Hariet Judnick remarks that the opt-in model is actually a better from a marketing standpoint, as well as a privacy standpoint. Reason being, if you have people who have shown an interest by opting-in, those individuals are very hot leads, and should be pursued instead of preying off people who have no idea what's happening to them.

Lack of Consent and Blatant Trickery

Jason Catlett of Junk Busters states that the efforts of DoubleClick were a, "blatant bait and switch trick" because for four years DoubleClick said that they weren't going to identify you personally. Now they are admitting that they are going to identify you and profile you and sell your information for profit. He continues stating that, "the fact that DoubleClick is not disclosing the names of the companies who are feeding them consumers' names is a shameful hypocrisy. They are trying to protect the confidentiality of the violators of privacy."

As with the opt-in argument, the advocacy groups want DoubleClick to obtain consent prior to using the information. Prior to May 2000, DoubelClick stated, "we're not in a position to do that [force its members to get permission from consumers before exchanging addresses and matching up their offline and online shopping habits]. We would encourage everyone to have a full disclosure, and we are going to absolutely stick to the opt-out policy."

According to the attorney for Hariet Judnick, "even if DoubleClick provides warnings, such warnings give no protection to many unsophisticated Web surfers . . . one wrong click and the originally anonymous cookie becomes a window into that consumer's private life."

Better Form of Marketing

According to DoubleClick's strategy, most e-commerce sites act like "gumball machines, you go up, put your money in and hope you get what you want. The gun-ball machine doesn't know who you are, whether it's your first visit or the 50th time. That's exactly how the Web is operating today," said Kathy Biro, CEO of Strategic Interactive Group, Boston. This is what advertisers want to penetrate.

Ben Addoms, head of sales and marketing for Excite/At Home, also approves of access to this kind of information, stating, "Once you get customers to buy, how do you take care of them and get them to buy again?" Sites have overlooked keeping customers and have spent most of their time getting new customers. Peter Adams, CEO of Primary Knowledge says this shortcoming is because marketers have failed to better use information available: cost and time. It can cost more than $1 million a year to run a system to capture data intelligently. Time can be worth even more than money for high-flying start-ups flush with IPO cash. People don't have the time to do this.

According to Bridget McCarville, Advertising Manager, Chevrolet, "The combination of high quality sites within the network and the DoubleClick DART (Dynamic Advertising, Reporting & Targeting), technology has provided us with an accountable marketing tool." DART gives DoubleClick's customers a list of targeting criteria from which to choose in determining who sees a particular ad, and a level of advertising, then demonstrates extensive feedback on the performance of the ads.

What has DoubleClick done since then?

DoubleClick has taken a number of measures to change its approach to Privacy issues. They have expanded the privacy team creating a Privacy Department with a Chief Privacy Officer and a Vice President of Data

Protection. They developed a new privacy policy that emphasizes their opt-out position and clarifies the focus on developing consumer information policies that protect privacy with their customers and invited public review of their new privacy policy.

DoubleClick's new Chief Privacy Officer states that "data protection issues demand a strong understanding of international and domestic legislature. Our new team's specialized experience in this field is crucial for our continued growth and strength in this sector of the business." With this and other appointments, DoubleClick feels they are dedicated to assuring user privacy while delivering effective online advertising.

DoubleClick has spent a considerable amount of effort in emphasizing how they utilize the "post" method as opposed to the "get" method of access to information through servers. This method ensures enhanced protection of privacy. A five point privacy initiative – "Internet Privacy Education Campaign" was launched by DoubleClick in February 2000 sponsoring 50 million banner advertisements linking to www.privacychoices.org. They also issued the following statement: "DoubleClick has never and will never use sensitive online data in our profiles, it is DoubleClick's policy to only merge personally identifiable information with non-personally identifiable information for profiling, after providing clear notice and choice."

Status of Complaints and Lawsuits

On January 22, 2001 the FTC closed investigation against DoubleClick for its data collection practices finding no violation of federal laws. On March 30, 2001 a Federal Judge dismissed all federal privacy suits against DoubleClick in New York, stating "Plaintiff's Amended Complaint fails to plead violations of any of the three federal statutes under which they bring suit." General Counsel for DoubleClick states "the groundbreaking decision marks the first time a court has interpreted these statutes in the context of Internet advertising."

On June 6, 2001, the Marin County Court denied the Demurrer filed by DoubleClick and allowed the case to proceed to trial on January 2002. The difference from the New York Court to the California court is that the California Constitution gives consumers protection against privacy-invasive acts by private entities. As a result, Amazon.com was sued as a subsidiary and even settled in a similar case for trying to match identities to data. They paid $40 to each individual in their 500,000 person database, as the case was a class action lawsuit.

The nature and scope of privacy issues faced by DoubleClick call into question a number interesting issues. Did DoubleClick engage in ethical practices when they decided to merge the databases? Could they have handled the situation differently? Clearly a lack of privacy and confidentiality considerations resulted in DoubleClick suffering in terms of their image and customer perception. Would it have been possible for DoubleClick to balance security and privacy needs with their profitability objectives? Now that Google has taken the company over, what are the implications?

Bibliography

Chapter 1

Knowledge@Wharton (2012) In the Middle East, cyberattacks are flavored with political rhetoric. Managing technology. Retrieved from http://knowledge.wharton.upenn.edu/arabic/article.cfm?articleid=2774. Excerpt reproduced with permission.

CBS News (2013) South Korea says North Korea behind computer crash in March. Retrieved from http://www.cbsnews.com/8301-205_162-57578853/south-korea-says-north-korea-behind-computer-crash-in-march/

Cusick, J. (2012) China telecoms giant could be cyber-security risk to Britain. The Independent. Retrieved from http://www.independent.co.uk/news/uk/politics/china-telecoms-giant-could-be-cybersecurity-risk-to-britain-8420432.html

Dhillon, G. (2001) Violation of safeguards by trusted personnel and understanding related information security concerns. Computers & Security, 20(2), 165-172.

DHS (2012) ICS-CERT Monitor. Retrieved from http://icscert.uscert.gov/pdf/ICSCERT_Monthly_Monitor_Oct-Dec2012.pdf

Economist (2012) The company that spooked the world. Retrieved from http://www.economist.com/node/21559929

Lew, J. (2010) Memorandum for the heads of executive departments and agencies. (memorandum). Retrieved from http://goo.gl/sry5eV

Symantec. (2012) Internet Security Report. Mountain View, California: Symantec. Retrieved from http://www.symantec.com/content/en/us/enterprise/other_resources/b-istr_main_report_2011_21239364.en-us.pdf

Chapter 2

Catalano, S. (2012) Stalking victims in the United States – revised. U.S. Department of Justice, Bureau of Justice Statistics. Retrieved from http://bjs.gov/content/pub/pdf/svus_rev.pdf

CBS 8. (2011) Man convicted of cyberstalking to undergo psychiatric evaluation before sentencing. Retrieved from

http://www.cbs8.com/story/15859709/cyberstalker-to-be-sentenced-in-san-diego.

FBI. (n.d.). Identity Theft. The Federal Bureau of Investigation. Retrieved from http://www.fbi.gov/about-us/investigate/cyber/identity_theft

FBI. (n.d.). Social Networking sites: Online friendships can mean offline peril. The Federal Bureau of Investigation. Retrieved from http://www.fbi.gov/about-us/investigate/vc_majorthefts/innocent/social-networking-sites

FTC. (2007) FTC releases survey of identity theft in the U.S. study shows 8.3 million victims in 2005. Federal Trade Commission. Retrieved from http://www.ftc.gov/opa/2007/11/idtheft.shtm

Garcia, C. (2013) Edcouch family arrested for cyber-stalking murdered in-law. Retrieved from http://www.valleycentral.com/news/story.aspx?id=932632.

Ginty, M. (2011) Cyberstalking Turns Web Technologies into Weapons. Retrieved from http://womensenews.org/story/crime-policylegislation/110501/cyberstalking-turns-web-technologies-weapons.

Lenhart, A. & Madden, M. (2007) Social networking websites and teens. Pew Research Center. Retrieved from http://

www.pewinternet.org/Reports/2007/Social-Networking-Websites-and-Teens.aspx

Martinez, S.M. (2004) Testimony before the House Government Reform Committee's Subcommittee on Technology, Information Policy, Intergovernmental Relations and the Census. Retrieved: http://www.fbi.gov/news/testimony/identity-theft-and-cyber-crime

Science Daily. (2013, February 12). New study examines victims and cyberstalking.   Science Daily. Sam Houston University. Retrieved from http://www.sciencedaily.com/releases/2013/02/130212075454.htm

Stalking resource center. 2012. The National Center for Victims of Crime.   Retrieved from http://www.victimsofcrime.org/our-programs/stalking-resource-center

Chapter 3

Santayana, G. (1905) Life of Reason: The phases of human progress. Vol. 1, Chapter 12. Retrieved from http://www.gutenberg.org/cache/epub/15000/pg15000.txt

Kleinberg, J. (2007) Computing: The wireless epidemic. Nature, 449(7160), 287-288.

US-CERT. (n.d.) United States Computer Emergency Readiness Team. Department of Homeland Security.   Retrieved from https://www.us-cert.gov/

Chapter 4

Beckman, J. (1997) Oil Industry Fraud. Evidence of contract fixing worries North Sea producers. Offshore Magazine. Retrieved from http://www.offshore-mag.com/articles/print/volume-57/issue-1/departments/drilling-production/oil-industry-fraud-evidence-of-contract-fixing-worries-north-sea-producers.html

CPNI. (2005) Targeted trojan email attacks. Centre for the Protection of National INfrastructure. Retrieved from http://goo.gl/zXDW0b

Crane, A. (2005) In the company of spies: When competitive

intelligence gathering becomes industrial espionage. Business Horizons, 48(3), 233-240.

Dhillon, G., & Chapman, S. (2006) To opt-in, or to opt-out? That is the question. A Case Study. Journal of Information System Security, 2(2), 46-55.

Javers, E. (2010) Broker, Trader, Lawyer, Spy: The secret world of corporate espionage. New York: Harper-Collins.

Panetta, L.E. (2012)   Remarks by Secretary Panetta to the Business Executives for National Security, New York City. Retrieved from http:// www.defense.gov/transcripts/transcript.aspx?transcriptid=5136

Schiller, C., & Binkley, J. R. (2011) Botnets: The killer web applications. Syngress.

Chapter 5

Menezes, A. J., Van Oorschot, P. C., & Vanstone, S. A. (2010) Handbook of applied cryptography. CRC press.

Chapter 6

Baskerville, R., & Dhillon, G. (2008) Information Systems Security Strategy: A Process View. In D. W. Straub, S. Goodman & R. Baskerville (Eds.), Information Security: Policy, Processes, and Practices. Armonk, NY: M E Sharpe.

Dhillon, G. (1997) Managing information system security. London: Macmillan.

Dhillon, G. (1998) Choosing appropriate organizational controls: managing the information assets. In M. Khosrowpour (Ed.), Effective utilization and management of emerging information technologies (pp. 473-477). Hershey PA: Idea Group Publication.

InstantSecurityPolicy.com. (n.d.) The IT Security Policy Guide: Why you need one, what it should cover, and how to implement it. Retrieved from http://goo.gl/i9LWZK

Kayworth, T., & Whitten, D. (2010) Effective Information Security

Requires a Balance of Social and Technology Factors. MIS Quarterly Executive, 9(3).

Chapter 7

Denning, D. E. (2000) Cyberterrorism: Testimony before the Special Oversight Panel on Terrorism Committee on Armed Services US House of Representatives (Vol. 23). Washington, May.

Haeni, R. E. (1997) Information warfare: An introduction. The George Washington University Cyberspace Policy Institute. Washington, D.C.: George Washington University. Retrieved from http://www.trinity.edu/rjensen/infowar.pdf

Kim, J. T., & Hyun, T. (2007) Status and Requirements of Counter-Cyberterrorism. World Academy of Science, Engineering and Technology, 620-623

Libicki, M. (1995) Chapter 1. What is information warfare? National Defense University. Washington, D.C.: Information Warfare Site. Retrieved from http://goo.gl/q8wJwi

Nelson, B., Choi, R., Iacobucci, M., Mitchell, M., & Gagnon, G. (1999) Cyberterror: Prospects and implications. Center for the Study of Terrorism and Irregular Warfare. Monterey, CA: United States Navy Naval Postgraduate School. Retrieved from http://www.au.af.mil/au/awc/awcgate/nps/cyberterror_prospects.pdf

President's Commission on Critical Infrastructure Protection. (1997) Critical foundations: Protecting America's Infrastructures. Federation of American Scientists. Retrieved from http://www.fas.org/sgp/library/pccip.pdf

TV Novosti. (2013, April 17) FBI: Cyber attacks – America's top terror threat. RT: Question More. Retrieved from http://rt.com/news/cyber-fbi-security-mueller-691/

Chapter 8

Access Data. (2003) Forensic Toolkit. Retrieved February 4, 2005, from http://www.accessdata.com/Product04_Overview.htm

Arthur, K. K. (n.d.) An Investigation Into Computer Forensic Tools. Retrieved February 8, 2005, from http://goo.gl/76pez0

Carrier, B. (n.d.) Open Source Digital Forensics Tools. Retrieved February 7, 2005, from http://goo.gl/ockG8p

Casey, E. (2000) Digital Evidence and Computer Crime (Second Edition). San Diego, CA: Academic Press.

CyberSecurity Institute. (2004) Code of Ethics and Conduct. Retrieved February 14, 2005, from http://goo.gl/VLreK8

Farmer, D; Venema, W. (2005) Forensic Discovery. Addison-Wesley Professional.

Guidance Software. (2005) EnCase Enterprise Edition. Retrieved February 4, 2005, from http://www.encase.com/products/ee_index.asp

IACIS. (n.d.) Forensic Procedures. Retrieved February 6, 2005, from www.iacis.com/html/procprint.htm

Isner, J. D. (2003) Computer Forensics: An Emerging Practice in the Battle Against Cyber Crime. Retrieved February 8, 2005, from http://goo.gl/hp53IX

Paraben Corporation. (2005) Paraben Forensic Tools. Retrieved February 4, 2005, from http://www.paraben-forensics.com/catalog/

Radcliff, D. (2002) Cybersleuthing Solves the Case. Retrieved February 9, 2005, from http://www.computerworld.com/securitytopics/security/story/0,10801,67299,00.html

Radeck, S. (n.d.) Forensic Techniques: Helping Organizations Improve Their Responses to Information Security Incidents. Computer Security Division, The National Institute of Standards and Technology. Retrieved from http://www.itl.nist.gov/lab/bulletns/bltnsep06.htm

Robbins, J. (n.d.) An Explanation of Computer Forensics. Available at http://www.computerforensics.net/forensics.htm

SearchSecurity.com Definitions. (2005) Retrieved February 2, 2005, from http://searchsecurity.techtarget.com/sDefinition/ 0,,sid14_gci1007675,00.html

Solomon, Michael G., Barrett, Diane and Broom, Neil. (2005) Computer Forensics Jump Start. San Francisco: Sybex.

The DIBS Group. (2004) The DIBS Methodology. Retrieved February 5, 2005, from http://www.dibsusa.com/methodology/ methodology.html

Chapter 9

Aristotle, (1953) The Nichomachean Ethics, J Harper, translator, Baltimore, MD: Penguin Books

Freeman, R. Edward, (1984) Strategic Management: A Stakeholder Approach Boston: Pittman

Mill, John Stuart and Jeremy Bentham, (1987) Utilitarianism and Other Essays Alan Ryan, editor London: Penguin Books,

Rawls, John, (1971) A Theory of Justice Cambridge, Mass.: Harvard University Press

Wilson, James Q, (1993) The Moral Sense New York: Free Press

Moores, T and Gurpreet Dhillon (2000) Software Piracy: a view from Hong Kong. Communications of the ACM. Vol 43, No 12.

Chapter 10

Athey, S. (1990) "A Comparison of the Fortune 500 and AACSB-Accredited Universities' Software Copying Policies," *CIS Educator Forum*, 2:4, 2-11.

Bartlett, C. A., & S. Ghosal (1987) "Managing Across Borders: New Organizational Responses," *Sloan Management Review*, 29:1, 43-53.

Bloombecker, J. J. B. (1991) "Computer Ethics: An Antidote to Despair,"

The Mid-Atlantic Journal of Business, 27:1, 33-42.

Campbell, R. (1984) Testimony before Congress on Computer and Communications Security and Privacy. Committee on Science and Technology, Subcommittee on Transportation, Aviation and Materials, US House of Representatives, 98th Congress, 2nd Session.

Cash, J. I., McFarlan F. W., McKenney J. L. & Applegate L. M., (1992) *Corporate Information Systems Management, Third Edition,* Homewood, IL: Irwin, 88-569.

Cohen, E. B., & Cornwell L., "Teaching Information Systems Ethics: A Study," *Proceedings of the 1994 IACIS Annual Conference, 26-31.* Washington, DC: International Association for Computer Information Systems.

Cohen, E., & Cornwell L. (1989) "A Question of Ethics: Developing Information Systems Ethics," *Journal of Business Ethics,* 8:6, 431-437.

Cohen, E., & Cornwell L. (1989) "College Students Believe Piracy is Acceptable," *CIS Educator Forum,* 2-5.

Couger, J. D. (1989) "Preparing IS Students to Deal with Ethical Issues," *MIS Quarterly,* 13:2, 211-218.

Davis, D. L., & Vitell S. J. (1992) "The Ethical Problems, Conflicts and Beliefs of Small Business Information Personnel," *The Journal of Computer Information Systems,* 22:4, 53-57.

Denning, D. E. and et al (1992), "The United States vs. Craig Neidorf: A Debate on Electronic Publishing, Constitutional Rights and Hacking," *Communications of the ACM,* 34:3, 23-43.

Drucker, P. F. (1998) "The Coming of the New Organization," *Harvard Business Review,* 66:1, 45-53.

Egelhoff, W. G. (1991) "Information Processing Theory and the Multinational Enterprise," *Journal of International Business Studies,* 22:3, 341-368.

Gopal, R. D., & Sanders G. L. (2000) "Global Software Piracy: You can't get Blood out of a Turnip," *Communications of the ACM,* 43:9, 83-89.

Im, J. H., & Van Epps P. D. (1991) "Software Piracy and Software Security in Business Schools: An Ethical Perspective," *Data Base,* 15-21.

Ives, B., & Jarvenpaa S. L. (1991) "Applications of Global Information

Technology: Key Issues for Management," *MIS Quarterly,* 15:1, 33-49.

Karimi, J., & Konsynski B. R. (1991) "Globalization and Information Management," *Journal of Management Information Systems,* 7:4, 7-26.

Kreie, J., & Cronan T. P. (2000) "Making Ethical Decisions," *Communications of the ACM,* 43:12, 66-71.

Machan, T. R. (1991) "Teaching Business Ethics in an Academic Environment of Mistrust," *The Mid-Atlantic Journal of Business,* 27:1, 59-65.

McConnell International, (2000) "Cyber Crime . . . and Punishment? Archaic Laws Threaten Global Information," *www.mcconellinternational.com.*

Moores, T., & Dhillon G. (2000) "Software Piracy: A View from Hong Kong," *Communications of the ACM,* 43:12, 88-93.

Neumann, P. G. (1991) "Inside RISKS: Computers, Ethics and Values," *Communications of the ACM,* 34:7, 106.

Neumann, S. (1992) "Issues and Opportunities in International Information Systems," *International Information Systems,* 1:4, 1- 13.

Ohmae, K. (1989) "Managing in a Borderless World," *Harvard Business Review.*

Parker, D. B., Swope S.& Baker B. N. (1990) Ethical Conflicts in Information and Computer Science, Technology and Business, Wellesley, MA: QED Information Sciences.

Porter, L. W., & McKibbin L. E. (1988) Management Education and Development: Drift or Thrust into the 21st Century? New York: McGraw Hill.

Porter, M. E., & Millar V. E. (1979) "How Information Gives You Competitive Advantage," *Harvard Business Review,* 137- 145.

Reid, R. A., Thompson J. K., & Logsdon J. L. (1992) "Knowledge and Attitudes of Management Students Toward Software Piracy," *Journal of Computer Information Systems,* 23:1, 46-51.

Roche, E. M. (1992) Managing Information Technology in Multinational Corporations. New York: Macmillan.

Solomon, S. L., & O'Brien J. A. (1990) "The Effect of Demographic Factors on Attitudes Toward Software Piracy," *The Journal of Computer Information Systems,* 20:3, 40-45.

Stark, A. (1993) "What's the Matter with Business Ethics?" *Harvard Business Review,* 38-48.

Wickham, M., Plotnicki, J., & Athey, S. (1992) "A Survey of Faculty Attitudes Towards Personal Computer Software Copying," The *Journal of Computer Information Systems,* 22:4, 47-52.

Wood, W. A. (1993) "Computer Ethics and Years of Computer Use," *The Journal of Computer Information Systems,* 23:4, 23-27.

Wood, W. A., (1991) "A View of Computer Ethics by Managers and Students," *The Journal of Computer Information Systems,* 22:2, 7-10.

Chapter 11

Ellison, Craig. "Unwire Your Office." PC Magazine (vol 22, num. 18, 2003) 81.

Gillespie, G. (2003) "Are VPNs Safe for the Wild Wild Web? Health care organizations are   turning to Web-based virtual private networks.   But how much risk will CIOs   accept?" Health Data Management. 11. 54.

Korpman, Ralph A. (2002) "This is not your parents' security system: defining user roles and   creating audit trails in a HIPAA – compliant system are two critical steps to   successful compliance."   Health Management Technology. 16.

Mulder, James T. (2003) "Doctors Log In; Secure Web Sites Provide Remote Access To Patient   Records." The Post Standard. C1.

Nichols, R. and Panos L. (2002) Wireless Security: Models, Threats and Solutions. New York: McGraw Hill

PR Newswire. (2003) "Multi-Tech VPN Router Provides Secure Remote Access to   Patient   Data."

PR Newswire Europe. (2003) "Gemplus: Denver health employees use Gemplus smart cards to securely access hospital network."

Tanenbaum, A. (2003) Computer Networks. Upper Saddle River, NJ: Prentice Hall PTR

Walters, B. (2003) "Wired and wireless security: the latest ways to thwart hackers and protect   critical information." Meetings & Conventions

44.

"HIPAA Compliance: Major healthcare organizations adopt QualsGuard security   platform." Managed Care Weekly Digest. 24. 2 June 2003 http://www.newsrx.com

"Information Technology: Italian cardiology network to use E-ceptionist." Medical   Devices & Surgical Technology Week. 49. 29 June 2003. http://www.newsrx.com

Chapter 12

Dhillon, G and Chapman, S. (2006). To op-in, or to opt-out? That is the question. A case study. Journal of Information System Security. Vol 2, No 2.

About the Author

Dr. Gurpreet Dhillon is Professor of Information Systems in the School of Business, Virginia Commonwealth University, Richmond, USA. He holds a Ph.D. from the London School of Economics and Political Science, UK. His research interests include management of information security, ethical and legal implications of information technology. His research has been published in several journals including *Journal of Management Information Systems, Information Systems Research, Decision Support Systems, European Journal of Information Systems, Information Systems Journal Information & Management, Communications of the ACM, Computers & Security, and International Journal of Information Management* among others. Gurpreet has authored eight books including *Principles of Information Systems Security: text and cases* (John Wiley, 2007). He is also the Editor-in-Chief of the *Journal of Information System Security*. Gurpreet's research has been featured in various academic and commercial publications and his expert comments have appeared in the *Knowledge@Wharton, New York Times, USA Today, Business Week, NBC News*, among others. In 2013 Gurpreet also published his first poetry book – *The Inner Truth*.

www.ingramcontent.com/pod-product-compliance
Lightning Source LLC
Chambersburg PA
CBHW081522220326
41598CB00036B/6293